So much better...

Michael Guest

Books by the same author

Peace with God –

A study of the Atonement

So much better...

An exposition of the letter to the Hebrews

Geoffrey Mitchell

Acknowledgements

All Scripture quotations unless otherwise indicated are taken from the New King James Version®. Copyright © 1982 by Thomas Nelson. Used by permission. All rights reserved.

Scripture quotations marked (NIV) are taken from the Holy Bible, New International Version®, NIV®. Copyright © 1973, 1978, 1984, 2011 by Biblica, Inc.™ Used by permission of Zondervan. All rights reserved worldwide. www.zondervan.com The "NIV" and "New International Version" are trademarks registered in the United States Patent and Trademark Office by Biblica, Inc.™

Scripture quotations marked (ESV) are from the ESV® Bible (The Holy Bible, English Standard Version®), copyright © 2001 by Crossway, a publishing ministry of Good News Publishers. Used by permission. All rights reserved.

Scripture quotations marked (KJV) are taken from The Authorized (King James) Version. Rights in the Authorized Version in the United Kingdom are vested in the Crown. Reproduced by permission of the Crown's patentee, Cambridge University Press.

First published 2021

ISBN: 978-1-874508-34-2

(also available as an e-book ISBN: 978-1-874508-35-9)

Published by:

Dawn Christadelphian Publications
5 Station Road, Carlton, Nottingham, NG4 3AT, U.K.

Printed and bound in Great Britain

CONTENTS

PREFACE

Whilst on the face of it, the letter to the Hebrews is not addressed to us Gentiles, it is in fact intensely interesting to those who share the faith of Abraham and are part of the family of God. The letter shows how that Jesus, the firstborn Son of God, is in so many ways better than the Old Covenant by which Israel were intended to be led to revere their God and to see in a shadowy way the coming of the saviour.

The word 'better' occurs 12 times in the letter:

- Christ was **so much better** than the angels (hence the title of this book), and in Christ there was

    o   a better hope

    o   a better covenant which is established on better promises

    o   better sacrifices

    o   a better and enduring possession

    o   a better, that is, a heavenly country

    o   a better resurrection

The letter is also a source of many uplifting passages which are favourites of many of God's children. To mention a few:

- the role of the angels in ministering to those appointed to salvation (Heb. 1:14)

- Jesus, the priest, who through personal experience understands our humanity (Heb. 4:14–16)

- God's desire to convince our doubting nature by confirming His great promises with oaths, even though it is impossible for Him to lie (Heb. 6:13–20)

- the definition of faith and the real-life examples given (Heb. 11)

- the practical advice to keep our eyes fixed upon our leader and not to give way under trial because it is God's method of training His children whom He loves (Heb. 12:1–11)

- the description of Jesus as the great Shepherd of the sheep, through whose work we can be made complete (Heb.13:20)

This book began as a series of Bible class addresses given at the Bramerton ecclesia. Steve Irving suggested that the series had the makings of a book. With his help and direction this modest volume has come to pass, and my prayer is that it will be of use to some who zealously search for God and His reward to the faithful.

My thanks therefore to Steve for giving time to steer me in spite of editing the Ecclesial Magazine and a number of other books. I am also most grateful to Rachel Lowe for undertaking the proof reading and Emma Perfitt for designing the cover.

Above all, I thank God who moved His servant to write this wonderful letter for the huge encouragement of all who seek glory and immortality.

GGM
August 2021

INTRODUCTION

The letter to the Hebrews may seem more than a little academic to us Gentile 21st Century Christians. Frequently the reasoning appears to be quite abstruse and difficult to follow. We could wonder why it was written at all. But the Gospels and the Acts of the Apostles show that there was a major problem which Jesus and the apostles had to confront and correct.

Its very title *The letter to the Hebrews* shows that the problem was a Jewish one. All through the Gospels, Acts and the letters, Jewish scholars and lawyers opposed Jesus and his disciples. Jesus was an offence to them in many ways and, in that they were fulfilling the words of the prophets. As Stephen said :

> *'You stiff-necked and uncircumcised in heart and ears! You always resist the Holy Spirit; as your fathers did, so do you. Which of the prophets did your fathers not persecute? And they killed those who foretold the coming of the Just One, of whom you now have become the betrayers and murderers, who have received the law by the direction of angels and have not kept it.'* (Acts 7:51-53)

Jesus was that 'rock of offence' which made them stumble. He was, in their estimation an uneducated man from a despised town. Yet he had undeniable authority and power. Foolishly, they tried to ascribe that power to Beelzebub. To accept Jesus as the Messiah, son of Abraham, son of David and worst of all, Son of God and 'The Prophet' spoken of by Moses, was impossible. He was irritating in his practices and critical of their man-made traditions and their oral law.

But they could never get the better of him in an argument however deviously they tried to trap him. The only solution was to put him to death and remove the irritant permanently. This they did, but the resurrection confounded them yet again. There were far too many witnesses to the risen Lord to deny the fact. Matters became even more serious when one of their own number, a zealous and energetic prominent Pharisee, let them down by doing a somersault on the way to persecute Jesus' disciples in Damascus. He claimed to be the last to witness the risen Lord; he had seen him and heard him, transforming his hatred to intense gratitude.

We know from the Acts that many Jews in Jerusalem, including priests, had been baptised into Christ, to the fury of the orthodox establishment. Paul's letters show how far the influence of the Jews had spread and the letter to the Galatians is particularly forthright in trying to persuade Jewish Christians not to fall for their arguments. *'They zealously court you, but for no good; yes, they want to exclude you, that you may be zealous for them.'* (Gal. 4:17)

As anarchy grew in Judea and zealots of all shades were trying to gain support for a revolt against Rome, it would have seemed unpatriotic for Jewish Christians to stand aside from such seemingly worthy aims and, under pressure, overlook that it was contrary to the teaching of Jesus. Paul explained, however, that their citizenship was in heaven (Phil. 3:20) and that they should stand fast in Jesus. The cataclysmic event of the Roman siege of Jerusalem was fast approaching because of the ungovernable nature of the Jews. So, the days of vengeance which Jesus had prophesied would fall upon the very people who were putting pressure upon Jesus' followers to bring them back to the foundations of Judaism, as they saw it.

A revision course

This letter to the Hebrews was to give the Jewish Christians a revision course concerning faith in Jesus and to prevent them reverting to Moses under pressure from the nationalistic

Judaisers. Hence the reasoning in this letter sought to renew their faith in Jesus by showing just how superior he was in every way. He was superior to the prophets, for Jesus revealed the very character of God; he was superior to angels through whom the Law was given; superior to Moses the law-giver; superior to Joshua. He was superior to Aaron the High Priest, not only in the priesthood, but also the sanctuary. The New Covenant, of which he was the ratifying sacrifice, was superior to the old, for his sacrifice was so superior to that of bulls and goats. Finally, he was superior in faith and as a shepherd of the flock of God.

It would appear that the readers of the letter were extremely well read in the Old Testament Scriptures. Their knowledge of the word puts us Gentiles to shame with our easy access to the word of God, with our concordances and on-line aids. Maybe they had been brought up as children to learn and memorise large parts of Scripture. Access to the word would have been relatively difficult for them; to do so would mean visiting a synagogue. Cumbersome scrolls would have to be taken down and unrolled. There were no chapters and verses to help find a passage. Yet Paul, who I believe wrote the letter, could use spiritual shorthand in demonstrating the argument, and his readers would understand. We find phrases like this: *'the spirit in David said'*; *'the Holy Spirit said'*; *'It is written'* and so on. We do the same; we have to assume a degree of Bible knowledge when we talk among ourselves. If we did not, our discussions would be severely limited. Even so, the writer was far from satisfied with the knowledge possessed by his readers.

Writing of Melchizedek he said there was much he wanted to say to them, but because they had become so slow to understand it would be difficult to explain. Really by this time they should have become teachers of God's word but instead they needed to be taught the basics all over again. They were vulnerable to false teaching not being able to discern between right and wrong (Heb. 5:11–14).

So much better...

The Scriptures are full of exhortations about gaining knowledge, getting wisdom, searching for it avidly as Jesus put it in his parable, as if it were a pearl of great price. An allusion perhaps to Proverbs 2 where the principle could hardly be put more emphatically. Summarising the exhortation in that chapter we are instructed to:

- take God's words to heart

- value His commandments

- attune our ears to wisdom

- ask for clear perception

- cry out for discernment

- hunt for it as if it were silver

- search for it as for buried treasure.

If we do those things, we will discover the knowledge and wisdom of God.

Nonetheless, Paul seemed to depend upon them having a knowledge of Scripture which might put us to shame. To give an example of the Jewish readers' recollection of Old Testament Scripture: if, before the New Testament existed, one wanted to prove that Jesus was one with his brothers, where would we go to prove the point? Paul's proof text is in Heb. 2:13: *'I and the children which God has given me.'* He did not say where the text was to be found and, without looking in the margin for a cross reference, would we know where that brief statement is to be found? In fact, the marginal reference directs us to Isaiah 8:18. But even then, having found the reference and looked at its context, what has it to do with the case? On the face of it, it seems to be about Isaiah and his sons Shear-Jashub and Maher-Shalal-

Hash-Baz. But it is only by careful study and with the help of the New Testament that we can see that the subject is indeed Jesus!

Notwithstanding their familiarity with the Old Testament, they were growing confused about the relevance of the Law. An extract from Acts illustrates the point. Those of the Jerusalem ecclesia pointed out that there were thousands of Jewish Christians and all of them were staunch upholders of the Law. Yet they had heard that Paul was teaching Jewish Christians scattered among the Gentiles to turn from Moses, to give up circumcising their children and their way of life. To allay their fears it was proposed that Paul himself should show that he was a practising Jew by assisting some Jews with rites required under the Law. Paul complied and was seen in the Temple. (Acts 21:20–25): However, it led to such an uproar that Paul had to be rescued by the Roman commander of the Fort of Antonia. This began his long detention which ended in Rome.

Jewish Christians and the Law

Evidently, it was not wrong for Jewish Christians to keep the Law providing:

- they understood that Jesus had fulfilled all that the Law had foreseen in its shadowy and indistinct way and

- that in keeping the Law, they could never make themselves righteous before God unless it was mixed with faith in Him and the one the Law pointed to.

It is apparent that they were not being led astray by the elders of the ecclesia. On the contrary, Paul exhorts them three times in the letter to remember these elders as the ones who had taught them the gospel. He says, take note of the effect it had on their way of life and follow their examples in faithful living. At the time this letter was written Peter and James may still have been among those who ruled over the Jerusalem ecclesia but whoever they were, they were not at fault. Peter and James had written letters to Jewish Christians scattered abroad among the Gentiles, but Paul was writing from abroad to plead with the Jewish congregation in Jerusalem, just as he had sent letters dealing with the same problem to Rome, Galatia, Ephesus, Philippi, Thessalonica and Colossae. He knew that the day of God's vengeance was fast approaching, as Peter had written (2 Pet. 3:10). The day of the Lord would come unexpectedly, and the Jewish elements would fall apart and be consumed. That day was but a decade or so in the future.   AD 70

We know from experience how hard it can be to change traditions in an ecclesia. By which, I do not mean doctrine or the commands of Christ, but those matters which have been accepted as the decent and orderly way to do things because it is the way it has always been done. Imagine how difficult it would have been for a person brought up as a faithful adherent to the Jewish traditions. Jesus was scathing about those traditions. His authority was attested to by God through miracles, wonders and signs witnessed by crowds of people all over the land, but just as the Exodus generation quickly forgot the wonders they had seen and were led astray by falsehood, so can any generation. It is a vital exhortation repeated countless times in the Scriptures.

The letter, however, was addressed to Jewish Christians who had been convinced that Jesus of Nazareth, a man coming from that despised town, the man condemned to death by officialdom, had certainly died on the cross and was indisputably alive again. Now perhaps thirty or so years later they were having doubts during those febrile days before the rebellion against Roman rule and the destruction of Jerusalem and the Temple. Is that why the letter begins without the usual formalities and introduces Jesus in such resounding terms?

The letter was evidently written before the destruction of the temple and Jerusalem. The references in Hebrews 10:2 to the sacrifices continuing to be offered would have been an anachronism post AD 70. Whatever the reason for writing this letter, and whoever its author was, its value to Christians of all time is immense and is the inspired word of God which is able to make us wise unto salvation.

Who was the writer?

Naturally we are intrigued to know who the author of this letter was, especially as it is the only book in the New Testament in which the writer is not named. However, it is not material to the content of the letter. It is inspired by God and that is what is all important. But we are curious to know who it was that asked for prayers on his behalf. It seems to me that the author is Paul. I have been impressed by so many thoughts that are paralleled in Paul's letters and speeches in the Acts of the Apostles. He was not a member of the Jerusalem ecclesia but hoped to visit. Another point lending support to the identification of Paul as the author is the mention of *'our brother Timothy'*. Timothy is the only person extraneous to the theme of the letter to be mentioned. There are many references in the New Testament to Timothy; some are in Acts, but all the others are in Paul's letters. The reference in this letter would be the sole exception if it is not by Paul.

The authorship has been a subject for many theories; the fact remains that he was known to the recipients of the letter and that it was an urgent appeal to stop them going off the rails.

So, for brevity, I refer to Paul as the author rather than using such impersonal phrases as 'the writer says' or 'the author writes'.

1 THE GREATNESS OF THE SON OF GOD

AN EXPOSITION OF HEBREWS 1

> *'God, who at various times and in various ways spoke in time past to the fathers by the prophets, has in these last days spoken to us by His Son, whom He has appointed heir of all things, through whom also He made the worlds; who being the brightness of His glory and the express image of His person, and upholding all things by the word of His power, when He had by Himself purged our sins, sat down at the right hand of the Majesty on high, having become so much better than the angels, as He has by inheritance obtained a more excellent name than they.'* (Heb. 1:1-4)

The wonder of this first long sentence needs to be thought about. The Almighty Creator has spoken. Where would we be if He had not spoken? Perplexing questions such as the following would remain unanswered:

- why are we here?

- is there any purpose in living?

- are we to live a life of vanity chasing after the wind?

God answers mankind's unease so plainly in His word, giving hope and peace of mind to all who search diligently for it as for that pearl of great price.

That first sentence is packed with information about God's purpose through Jesus. Jesus is God's son, begotten by Him. God revealed His character in Jesus; Jesus is heir to the great promises of God and will save those who place their trust in Him. Those in him will be given righteousness and through him possess all things. As the word explains, when all has been perfected and God is all in all, it will have been done through Jesus. (Eph.1:9-11 Col 1:15-18)

The resurrected Jesus is shown to be second only to God in status, so great that the need to say any more seems unnecessary. Nonetheless, having started at this most elevated level Paul goes on to show that, of course, Jesus must be far superior to all other levels of life, including the angels. Old Testament proofs are brought forward to demonstrate the truth of this majestic first sentence by demonstrating that Jesus is the only begotten son of God. Jesus is obviously better than the angels, although, during his mortality a little lower. (Ps. 8)

Paul's argument appeals to reason and progresses by logical steps to show that Jesus is better in various ways, especially in matters related to the Mosaic order. Jesus is better than the High Priest; the New Covenant ratified through Jesus is better than the Old given through angels and we will notice many more examples as we proceed..

'Better' is an oft repeated word in this letter and is the translation of a Greek word, *kreisson*. It comes from a root word *kratos* which means 'more powerful', 'stronger'. 'Better' is a simple English word and is a good translation of the Greek, as a comparison with its use elsewhere in the New Testament will show.

Jesus' superiority over the angels

Why was this important? Because as Stephen had said, they had received the Law through the ministry of angels. Paul wrote that the Law had been established through angels to a mediator. (Gal. 3:19) Moses was the mediator who taught the Law to Israel. However, the seed promised to Abraham had now come and was far above all, the firstborn Son of God. The change from the law to the liberty now offered in Christ through faith was great and wonderful.

Jesus had been foreseen by the prophets and Paul illustrates that with some examples. The prophets had spoken of salvation through Jesus in many ways, but only in fragments. These were the hidden things which were now revealed. It was not new teaching; it was all there from Genesis to Malachi but no one prophet had the whole picture.

Jesus gave a wonderful lesson to the two on the way to Emmaus, explaining to their uncomprehending minds the meaning of the prophets' words which spoke of the suffering of the Messiah before his elevation to glory and immortality. And so he showed them all the Scriptures that referred to himself from Moses, the prophets and the Psalms (Luke 24:25–27).

But they were not alone in their lack of understanding. The prophets themselves also wanted to know what their words meant and how and when they would be fulfilled. Even the angels longed to know more. The two disciples on the way to Emmaus had received that wonderful revelation from the Messiah himself. Jesus had already said at the Last Supper that when he had gone away, he would send them the Holy Spirit which would remind them of all the things he had taught them but had not understood (1 Pet 1:10–12).

Now these mysteries had been revealed to the angels and to the Jews by the Holy Spirit sent by Jesus from heaven to the apostles and those elders to whom the Spirit had been given. Those mysteries were also revealed to all nations through Paul and others as ministers of the New Covenant (2 Cor. 3:6) and was also being written down by men moved by the Holy Spirit, fulfilling Jesus' promise. *'The Helper, the Holy Spirit, whom the Father will send in My name, He will teach you all things, and bring to your remembrance all things that I said to you.'* (John 14:26)

The opening paragraph of the letter to the Hebrews ended with the amazing news that Jesus had *'sat down at the right hand of the Majesty on high, having become so much better than the angels, as He has by inheritance obtained a more excellent name than they.'*

The excellent name

What is that name? Paul elaborates in the letter to Philippians (2:9–11). It is a name above all other names, a name before whom all should bow, be they in heaven or on earth. All should confess that Jesus Christ is Lord, thus giving glory to God his Father.

When preaching in the synagogue at Antioch in Pisidia, Paul seems to imply that it was after his resurrection that Jesus became God's son in the complete sense. Jesus no longer bore Adam's nature; he was now immortal, having been raised to the divine nature of his Father and given his Father's name. The name was bestowed on him as the firstborn son, the only begotten son and that name could be no higher. So Paul said all this had been promised to the fathers of the nation and had now been fulfilled in their lifetime. So he quoted Psalm 2: *'You are my son, today I have begotten you.'*

Paul also wrote in his letter to the Colossians about the pivotal role Jesus has in the purpose of his Father. He said that he is the image of the invisible God. We observe that Adam had been created in the image of God but had ruined himself, bringing the curse upon him and all his descendants. Jesus showed us to perfection what a man made in the image of God was like. In raising him to the divine nature, Jesus became the first born of a new creation. Everything about that new creation is held together in him. He is the head of the body, the ecclesia. Through him, reconciliation has been made possible between God and man thus creating peace (Col 1:15–19).

Furthermore, no angel had been given the honour of sitting at the right hand of the Majesty on high. Even Gabriel, in admonishing Zacharias said: *'I am Gabriel, who stands in the presence of God.'* (Luke 1:19)

The next point in the argument is: - *'For to which of the angels did He ever say: "You are My son, today I have begotten You"?'* (Heb. 1:5) This proof from the second Psalm is potent; it speaks of the opposition to God's son and the irresistible will of God to place His son on His throne in Zion and to subdue the nations before him. At the time of the writing of this letter, that opposition was virulent as illustrated by the following historical account.

When Peter and John had been arrested and imprisoned, it was because the Jewish rulers were enraged by the apostles' insistence in preaching Jesus Christ, alive again in spite of his execution by the same Jewish rulers. Upon their miraculous release from prison the disciples saw the relevance of Psalm 2 to the situation. The rulers were indeed raging against the Lord and His Christ. So they said *'Lord, you are God, who made heaven and earth and the sea, and all that is in them, who by the mouth of Your servant David have said: "Why did the nations rage, and the people plot vain things? The kings of the earth took their stand, and the rulers were gathered together against the Lord and against his Christ."'* (Act 4:24–26)

The next proof (Heb. 1:5) is also powerful. It is a quotation from the covenant God made with David and was a key prophecy in the expectation that the Messiah would come from David's descendants and rule Israel forever. Their hope was that he would deliver them from Roman oppression; they did not understand that the Messiah was much more than David's son but was God's son also. The significance of the words of the covenant were now obvious to all who believed when God said: *'I will be to him a Father, and he shall be to me a son.'*

Let all the angels of God worship him

The next proof (Heb. 1:6) is quite obscure. *'But when He again brings the firstborn into the world, He says: "Let all the angels of God worship him."'* Where does this verse come from? Marginal references steer us to Deuteronomy 32:43 which is the last verse of Moses' song: *'Rejoice, O Gentiles, with His people; For He will avenge the blood of His servants, And render vengeance to His adversaries; He will provide atonement for His land and His people.'* Although angels are not mentioned in this passage, many translations assert that the quotation is taken from the Septuagint and this is also supported by the Dead Sea Scrolls. The 'New English Translation of the Septuagint' renders the passage *'Be glad, O nations with his people, and let all the angels of God prevail for him.'*

Paul precedes his quotation from Deuteronomy by saying *'But when He again brings the firstborn into the world.'* We might have assumed that this passage was referring to the praises of the angels in the presence of the shepherds outside Bethlehem. However, they were praising God not Jesus, and the word 'again' indicates a second bringing of Jesus into the world; not his birth but his resurrection, which Psalm 2 alludes to in saying *'You are my son, today I have begotten you.'*

Returning to the proof from Deuteronomy 32:43, the context is important for, as already observed, the words come at the very end of the Song of Moses. That song was almost Moses' last exhortation to Israel. He was to die later that very day when the Children of Israel were on the threshold of the Promised Land. So it was Moses' last opportunity to exhort Israel: *'... and he said to them: "Set your hearts on all the words which I testify among you today, which you shall command your children to be careful to observe--all the words of this law. For it is not a futile thing for you, because it is your life, and by this word you shall prolong your days in the land which you cross over the Jordan to possess."'* (Deut. 32:46–47)

The song of Moses is prophetic but also historic. As is so often the case with Scripture, it speaks of things yet to happen as if they have already happened. God who sees all things in His purpose knows the end from the beginning. The song addresses Israel as the heavens and the earth upon which His word is likened to the rain and dew which should bring forth fruits from the earth. Instead, they corrupted themselves. The LORD, their Rock had made them to be His special people, His portion, the apple of His eye. He cared for them, encircled them, carried them in His arms and instructed them, only to be scorned by them by turning to gods of their own making. So, the LORD saw it and spurned them. He said: *'I will hide my face from them.'* He would make the memory of them to cease from among men. Yet He did not, lest their enemies should claim the credit and say *'Our hand is high; it is not the LORD who has done this.'* Israel is a nation void of understanding. Yet for all this *'The LORD will judge His people and have compassion on His servants.'* And so, the song concludes: *'Rejoice, O Gentiles, with His people; For He will avenge the blood of His servants, and render vengeance to His adversaries; He will provide atonement for His land and His people.'* (Deu 32:43)

To understand this as a reference to Jesus Christ, we need to be informed by the whole of the word of God. Jesus is not identified in this proof. But who is it that the LORD would raise up to avenge the blood of His enemies and provide atonement for His land and people? In the broadest sense the greatest enemy is death. The Gospel of Salvation begins in Genesis 3:15 and concludes in Revelation with the last enemy, death, being destroyed. All of this is accomplished through Jesus.

At Moses' death their knowledge would have been limited to the Pentateuch, but much was revealed about God's scheme for the salvation of the faithful. They could have learned about:

- the seed of the woman who would crush the serpent's head

- the seed of Abraham through whom all families of the earth would be blessed; that seed would possess the gate of his enemies

- the sceptre, which would not depart from Judah

- the Shepherd and stone of Israel

- the blessing upon Joseph

- Balaam's fourth prophecy: the star to come out of Jacob who would batter the brow of Moab and destroy the sons of tumult, and out of Jacob One shall have dominion

- the prophet like unto Moses of Deuteronomy 18: *'I will put My words in his mouth, and he shall speak to them all that I command him.'*

The Law taught them crucial matters albeit in a shadowy way.

The Hebrew scholars in Jerusalem, in reading the proof: *'Rejoice, O Gentiles, with His people'* would have known all that and more besides because they knew its context. Indeed, the Song of Moses is a quarry of material quoted throughout the Old and New Testaments. All this knowledge revealed in the books of Moses should have stung them into revising their thinking and to repent of their rejection of the Christ.

Things hidden in the Old Testament.

Thinking about the difficulties we have in understanding some of the Old Testament proof texts that are quoted in the letters of the New Testament, we need to remember that these things were hidden until God chose to reveal them. As Paul wrote: *'We speak the wisdom of God in a mystery, the hidden wisdom which God ordained before the ages for our glory.'* He adds that had the rulers of this age known these things they would not have crucified the Lord of glory! He goes on to say: *'But God has revealed them to us through his spirit.'* (1 Cor. 2:7–8, 10) This is just what Jesus promised the apostles when he said that the Holy Spirit would teach them all things (John 16:13–15).

So, we have the great blessing of the New Testament which opens our eyes to see things about which we would otherwise be in the dark. It is also true that without the Old Testament there would be no foundation for the teaching of the New.

Jesus' superiority over the angels

The next proofs brought forward to show Jesus' superiority over the angels are relatively straightforward. He quotes two Psalms to show that the angels are servants or ministers, whereas Jesus is a king and his throne will last forever.

The two Psalms conflated here are Psalms 45 and 104. Psalm 104 begins *'Bless the LORD O my soul'*; v. 4 continues: *'Who makes His angels spirits, His ministers a flame of fire.'* The servant-role of the angels is in contrast to the royal status of Jesus as expressed in Psalm 45:6–7. *'Your throne, O God, is forever and ever; A scepter of righteousness is the scepter of your kingdom. You love righteousness and hate wickedness; Therefore God, Your God, has anointed you with the oil of gladness more than Your companions.'* Jesus' companions are his brothers and sisters, the children of God; more is said about them in Hebrews chapter 2.

The Hebrew Christians knew full well that God had raised Jesus to glory and immortality and that he had ascended to the right hand of the Father. It is also possible that they had already heard of *'The revelation of Jesus Christ, which God gave him to show to his servants...'* Therein are many descriptions of Jesus' status. For example: *'Jesus Christ, the faithful witness, the firstborn from the dead, and the ruler over the kings of the earth.' 'King of kings and Lord of Lords'* etc. (Rev. 1:5)

It is interesting to notice the type in David as one who was anointed more, or above, his fellows. It was not thought worthwhile to call David off the hills to meet the great judge and prophet Samuel, and yet it was David who was anointed above his brothers to be the shepherd of the flock of God!

The Jewish authorities never accepted Jesus as the anointed of God, the Messiah. Yet, although he was despised by men he was raised to sit with his Father on His throne. The same prospect is promised to believers, providing they overcome. '*To him who overcomes I will grant to sit with me on my throne, as I also overcame and sat down with my Father on his throne.*' (Rev. 3:21)

The reason for Jesus being anointed above his fellows is obvious. He loved righteousness and hated iniquity. Because he was perfect in these matters, God raised him to immortality. Without that perfection, a sinless life totally devoted to his Father's will, we would have no hope of salvation. It is only by believing that Jesus died for our sins and that God raised him from the tomb that we can be counted righteous! We read that '*... Christ Jesus, who became for us wisdom from God – and righteousness and sanctification and redemption.*' (1 Cor. 1:30) No wonder '*Therefore God, Your God, has anointed you with the oil of gladness more than Your companions.*'

Having extolled the majesty of Christ and his everlasting kingdom, Paul goes on to show that there is a heavens and earth which will not endure but perish.

> '*You, Lord, in the beginning laid the foundation of the earth, and the heavens are the work of your hands. They will perish, but you remain; and they will all grow old like a garment; like a cloak you will fold them up, and they will all be changed but you are the same, and your years will not fail.*' (Heb. 1:10–12)

These words are a quotation from Psalm 102:25–28; neither Paul or the Psalmist can be referring to the physical heavens and earth, because Scripture declares: '*One generation passes away, and another generation comes; But the earth abides forever.*' (Ecc 1:4 Jer.31:35,36. Jer.33:25,26)

So much better...

Before examining this difficult passage from Psalm 102 we will prepare the way with a brief look at the metaphor of the heavens and earth in Scripture.

Heavens and earth – a metaphor for Israel

Here are a few examples of the metaphor 'heavens and the earth'.

- Abraham's seed is likened to the stars for multitude.

- Joseph's dream of the sun, moon and stars bowing down to him was understood by Jacob to mean himself and his family.

- Deuteronomy 10:22 says: *'Your fathers went down to Egypt with seventy persons, and now the LORD your God has made you as the stars of heaven in multitude.'*

- The Song of Moses (Deut. 32) begins by Moses addressing all the assembly of Israel like this: *'Give ear O heavens, and I will speak; and hear, O earth, the words of my mouth. Let my teaching drop as the rain...'*

- The metaphor about the rain and dew is used in Isaiah 55 *'So shall my word be that goes forth from my mouth...'*

- The prophecy of Isaiah begins like the Song of Moses *'Hear O heavens, and give ear O earth! For the LORD has spoken'* (Isa.1:2) and goes on to describe the sinful nation of Israel.

- Jeremiah uses the same metaphor: *'Has a nation changed its gods, which are not gods? But My people have changed their Glory For what does not profit. Be astonished, O heavens, at this, and be horribly afraid; be very desolate," says the LORD.'* (Jer. 2:11,12)

- Jesus used the same figure: *'Immediately after the tribulation of those days the sun will be darkened, and the moon will not give its light; the stars will fall from heaven, and the powers of the heavens will be shaken.'* (Mat.24:29)

These are just a sample of many which the Hebrew Christian readers would have known.

So, we return to Psalm 102. What beginning is meant? What earth and heavens were to grow old and perish, to be put away like an old garment? This is contrasted with 'you', who remain unchanged, 'you' who do not grow old or wear out. Who is this?

The source of this proof is Psalm 102:25–27. The heading of this Psalm is 'The prayer of an afflicted man. When he is faint and pours out his lament to the LORD.'

It seems to be a Messianic Psalm revealing Jesus' thoughts during his ministry to Israel: the trials he endured, the hatred, the loneliness, the threats upon his life, the physical wear and tear and mental exhaustion from teaching and refuting the many challenges from the scribes and Pharisees. So great was the pressure upon him that he even forgot to eat (Ps. 102:4). Indeed, this gave his family anxiety (Mark 3:20–21). So the afflicted man of this Psalm complains *'Because of your indignation and your wrath; for you have lifted me up and cast me away.'* (Ps.102:10) Jesus was human and such thoughts may well have crossed his mind. Isaiah 53 tells us of the suffering endured by Jesus for our sakes: *'smitten by God, and afflicted... he was wounded for our transgressions... The LORD laid on him the iniquity of us all.'* Psalm 102 ought therefore to have prompted introspection and a recall of the sufferings of Jesus on their behalf.

The afflicted man of Psalm 102 continues by lamenting the brevity of his life and yet by comparison *'You LORD shall endure for ever'*. But then the mood of the Psalm changes and becomes full of anticipation. The time has arrived for mercy to be shown to Zion, so that the nations will fear the LORD, because he is going to build up Zion and appear in her in glory. The LORD looked down on the misery of the captive and set free those doomed to death. Nations and kingdoms will be united in their worship of the LORD. The work of Jesus as the saviour, was to proclaim the name of the LORD, the gospel of the kingdom of God and salvation. Then the Psalm returns to lament Jesus' suffering, that his days were so short. He pleads not to be taken away in the middle of his life (he died at about half the allotted span of three score years and ten) when you LORD live forever. Isaiah 53 reiterates such thoughts as does that great Messianic Psalm 22 which also begins in complaint but ends in complete confidence in God.

The founding of the Israelite heavens and earth

Now we come to the proof quoted in Heb.1:10 - *'Of old You laid the foundation of the earth, And the heavens are the work of Your hands.'* (Psalm 102:25) We have looked briefly at a few examples where 'heavens and earth' and 'sun, moon and stars' are figures of Israel. The LORD laid the foundation of Israel as a nation at Mount Sinai. He declared that they would be His special people out of all nations and made a covenant with them. But that covenant was powerless to save them from death. All it could do was prolong their lives and give them wonderful blessings if they were faithful. It was powerless to save because Israel could not keep it in all its details. Therefore they fell under its curse. *'... the man who does them shall live by them.'* (Gal. 3:12) In due course the LORD removed that covenant which had become old and introduced a New Covenant. The Old Covenant, like an old coat would be discarded to be replaced by a new one. (Much is said about the New Covenant later in this letter.)

That however is not the end of the Psalm. Just as the LORD continues forever and his years have no end, so His servants' sons will have a permanent home and their descendants will always be in his presence, proclaiming the name of the LORD in Zion and his praise in Jerusalem. (Ps. 102:28) Thus everlasting life is promised for God's servants and their descendants through the forgiveness of sins made possible under the New Covenant.

Isaiah 51 speaks of a wonderful future for Israel, on the basis of faith rather than works. *'Listen to Me, you who follow after righteousness.'* (Isa 51:1)   This is compared with those who did not listen and consequently were walking in the dark (50:10). If so, the exhortation which follows is much to the point: *'You who seek the LORD: Look to the rock from which you were hewn, And to the hole of the pit from which you were dug. Look to Abraham your father, And to Sarah who bore you; For I called him alone, And blessed him and increased him.'* (Isa. 51:1–2) Abraham's faith was accounted to him for righteousness long before the Law was given.

> *'For the LORD will comfort Zion, He will comfort all her waste places; He will make her wilderness like Eden, And her desert like the garden of the LORD; Joy and gladness will be found in it, Thanksgiving and the voice of melody. Listen to Me, My people; And give ear to Me, O My nation: For law will proceed from Me, And I will make My justice rest As a light of the peoples. My righteousness is near, My salvation has gone forth, And My arms will judge the peoples; The coastlands will wait upon Me, And on My arm they will trust. Lift up your eyes to the heavens, And look on the earth beneath. For the heavens will vanish away like smoke, The earth will grow old like a garment, And those who dwell in it will die in like manner; But My salvation will be forever, And My righteousness will not be abolished. Listen to Me, you who know righteousness, You people in whose heart is My law.'* (Isa. 51:3–7)

This quotation is surely an allusion to the New Covenant in which God will write his laws upon their hearts. Isaiah continues with lovely words of comfort and hope, reminding them of God's mighty acts for them in the Exodus and how in the future the ransomed of the LORD will return to enter Zion with singing.

So, that quotation from Psalm 102 is extremely meaningful. Israel is to become a new heavens and a new earth. Peter writing of the removal of the old heavens and earth said: *'Nevertheless we, according to His promise, look for new heavens and a new earth in which righteousness dwell.'* (2 Pet. 3:13) It will be an Israel comprising Jews and Gentiles united in Christ (Eph. 2:11–13)

Ministering spirits

We come to the next point of evidence in demonstrating the superiority of Jesus. Referring to the angels he says: *'Are they not all ministering spirits sent forth to minister for those who will inherit salvation?'* (Heb. 1:14)

The implications of this verse are wonderfully comforting. Scripture has much to say about angels and their work as servants of God. We think of two examples: the angel sent to strengthen Jesus in his intense anguish in Gethsemane. This very personal ministration was of the utmost importance. What would have become of God's plan of salvation if Jesus had given way at that moment of extreme stress? That angelic ministration was vital to our salvation.

Another example is the angel's ministrations to Israel in Egypt. Psalm 78.49 speaks of God dealing with the Egyptians: *'He cast on them the fierceness of his anger, wrath, indignation, and trouble, by sending angels of destruction among them.'* From the Egyptian viewpoint these angels were evil in the extreme. Likewise, when Sennacherib fled back to his own land following a dreadful night when the angel of the LORD went out and struck down 185,000 in the camp of the Assyrians (2 Kings 19:35).

Even David was frightened by the angel who brought the plague on Israel after he had been moved by God to number the people. David's normal response would have been as Psalm 35: *'Let those be put to shame and brought to dishonor who seek after my life; Let those be turned back and brought to confusion who plot my hurt. Let them be like chaff before the wind, and let the angel of the LORD chase them. Let their way be dark and slippery, and let the angel of the LORD pursue them.'* (Psa. 35:4-6)

Psalm 103 expresses the same sentiments as the verse in Hebrews.1:14, i.e. the caring ministrations of God's angels for the everlasting wellbeing of God's servants. *'But the mercy of the LORD is from everlasting to everlasting on those who fear Him, and His righteousness to children's children, to such as keep His covenant and to those who remember His commandments to do them.'* (Ps. 103:17–18)

How is the steadfast love of the LORD exercised? *'Bless the LORD, you His angels, who excel in strength, who do His word, heeding the voice of His word. Bless the LORD, all you His hosts, you ministers of His, who do His pleasure.'* (Ps. 103:20–21)

The world of today deludes itself, thinking that it is controlling its own affairs, although at present that confidence is being severely shaken by the threats looming before it. In all the seemingly chaotic affairs of this world, the LORD's steadfast love is upon those that fear Him! It is the angels who act for Him in his rule over the kingdoms of men and who watch over us. (Ps. 103:19)

We do not see the angels, although some have on occasions been very aware of their help in an hour of need. For the most part we are like Elisha's servant at Dothan. As far as he could see, a great army of Syrians had surrounded the city in their hunt for Elisha. It appeared to be a time of great peril for Elisha and the young man. In reality it was nothing of the kind and the young man was taught a lesson which we must also take to heart. Elisha asked the LORD to open the young man's eyes and he saw the horses and chariots of fire all round Elisha. (2 Kings 6:17)

Psalm 34 proved to be true for Elisha's servant

Psalm 34 proved to be true for that young man because the LORD heard him and saved him from all his fears: *'The angel of the LORD encamps all around those who fear Him, and delivers them'.* (Ps. 34:7)

Notice how at Dothan, the presence of the LORD's angels is described: *'Horses and chariots of fire.'* These words have echoes elsewhere in Scripture. For example, the description seems to correspond in some details to the vision of the glory of the LORD as seen by Ezekiel.

- Below the throne of God were the cherubim, part of which consisted of wheels

- The spirit of the living creatures was in the wheels

- Their appearance was like burning coals of fire or torches

- The fire was bright and out of the fire went lightning

- The rims of the wheels were full of eyes, and they were under the direction of the one on the throne

Other examples are found in Ezekiel 10:2,6 and 2 Kings 2:11 and Psalm 18:8–15. We notice the similarity with God's ministers described in Hebrews.1:7: *'Who makes His angels spirits and his ministers a flame of fire.'* This is quoting Psalm 104: *'Who makes the clouds His chariot, who walks on the wings of the wind, who makes His angels spirits, His ministers a flame of fire.'* (Ps. 104:3–4)

Angels are not all powerful (Daniel 10:5, 6 and 13; Jude 1:9); nor all knowing (Matthew 24:36. 1 Peter 1:10-12). Despite this, we have been given enough evidence to convince us of the power of the message of Hebrews 1:14 that they are given the task of ministering to those who will receive an eternal inheritance in the kingdom of God.

Revelation 5:11 shows how close to our heavenly Father they are and also how numerous, for John heard the voices of ten thousand times ten thousand, and thousands of thousands of angels round about the throne. What greater comfort and reassurance could we wish for than to know that there are so many, some of whom are ministering to us personally?

Heirs of salvation

The Greek word translated 'ministering' implies a priestly role and is used in the Septuagint with regard to Aaron's ministrations in the Tabernacle. It is also related to the word 'deacon' as used in the King James' Version. The priests in Israel had a vital role in keeping the knowledge of God before the people and are referred to as God's ministers (Jer. 33:21). The angels' role as God's ministers is to serve those who will inherit salvation.

In the New Testament it is obvious that the word 'inherit' does not bear its common meaning which is to receive things promised in the will of a deceased person. If it did, we would ask, has anyone made a will and died and, for example, left us eternal life? The Greek scholar William Barclay helps unravel this puzzle when he wrote:

'The word inherit is quite common in the Gospels. For example, the rich young man said to Jesus: 'What must I do to inherit eternal life? (Mk 10.17) Here the NEB has 'to win'. There is a problem of translation here. In ordinary English to inherit is to enter into possession of something when its previous owner has died, and an inheritance comes to us on the death of its original possessor, who has left it to us. This is not the New Testament sense of the word at all. What it does mean in the New Testament is to enter into possession of that which has been promised by God, with the added implication that, since the promise has been made by God, the fulfilment of the promise is sure. The word 'inherit' should be dropped from translation because of the implications of the death of the testator. It is better to translate the rich young man's question thus; 'What am I to do to get this eternal life which God has promised?'

William Barclay translates Heb.1:14: - *'Clearly, the angels are serving spirits, despatched each on his own errand, to help those who are to receive the salvation which God has promised.'*

Vine also confirms that the common meaning of 'inherit' differs from New Testament usage. 'An heir,' Vine writes, is 'one to whom something has been assigned by God, on possession of which, however, he has not yet entered; as Abraham, (Rom 4:13,14) and of Christ (Heb 1:2).'

Even though we may not have noticed the semantic problem, our understanding has always been that 'inherit' in passages such as *'Blessed are the meek for they shall inherit the earth.'* (Matt. 5:5) means 'to possess'. It is interesting to observe that the New English Bible translators being aware of the problem translate 1 Corinthians 15:50 with 'possess' instead of 'inherit': *'What I mean brothers, is this: flesh and blood can never possess the kingdom of God, and the perishable cannot possess immortality.*

2 SALVATION THROUGH CHRIST

AN EXPOSITION OF HEBREWS CHAPTER 2

Exhortation

In view of all that has been said before, this is the exhortation: *'Therefore we must give the more earnest heed to the things we have heard, lest we drift away.'* (Heb. 2:1)

In the context of this letter the exhortation of verse 1 means to avoid being carried away by popular nationalism and to resist joining the patriotic crowd. Rather the recipients of the epistle should stand firm as disciples of Jesus, realising that their citizenship is a heavenly one (Phil. 3:20). To stand firm must have been hard, just as it was hard for brethren in the First and Second World Wars to seek exemption from military service and be regarded as traitors. The stand against Jewish nationalism was made harder by the apparent plausibility of the zealots' propaganda which was to return to the Law of Moses. It is ironical that the appeal of God's prophets for generations had been that the nation should return to the Law. Ever since the days of Moses, it should have been the centre of Jewish life, but it had frequently been forsaken for paganism. The great stumbling stone was Jesus Christ, who was indisputably alive and seated at the right hand of the Father.

So, the letter continues in verse 2: *'For if the word spoken through angels proved steadfast, and every transgression and disobedience received a just reward...'* Examples of such punishments are found in Numbers chapters 14, 16 and 25 where flagrant rebellion by Israel received just recompense. It is ironical that the Jews at the time of the writing of this letter, were, in fact, receiving 'just punishment' by suffering Gentile domination, and furthermore, 'the days of vengeance' or 'the time of punishment' would again soon fall upon them as prophesied by Jesus (Luke 21:22). Time and again in their history they had been punished for rebelling against God. Now something superior in every way had been offered them, only to be despised and rejected. So verse 3 continues *'... how shall we escape if we neglect so great a salvation, which at the first began to be spoken by the Lord, and was confirmed to us by those who heard Him, God also bearing witness both with signs and wonders, with various miracles, and gifts of the Holy Spirit, according to His own will?'*

The Lord himself, the Son of God, now seated at the right hand of God, had announced this great salvation with many miracles, wonders and signs. Many had witnessed these undeniable proofs of the authenticity of the message – it was from God – God who had spoken to us in these last days through His son, the son He had raised from the dead.

Not only had God borne witness to the message through Jesus by means of signs and wonders, with various miracles, but He had also distributed the gifts of the Holy Spirit to some of the disciples as well. Many of them would have known of such brothers and sisters and may even have been blessed with spirit gifts themselves, enabling them to edify and build up the ecclesias.

One would suppose that the memory of such great blessings could never grow dim, yet Israel's history shows otherwise. Again, and again Psalm 106 shows how quickly they forgot: *'They made a calf in Horeb, and worshiped the molded image. Thus they changed their glory into the image of an ox that eats grass. They forgot God their Saviour, who had done great things in Egypt, wondrous works in the land of Ham, awesome things by the Red Sea.'* (Ps. 106:19–22) Once more, they were in danger of forgetting the great salvation wrought for them in Christ by again becoming disciples of the Scribes and Pharisees, who Jesus had castigated as hypocrites (Matt. 23).

The great salvation
Again the letter focusses on the superiority of Jesus. The angels who had appeared to the patriarchs, and to Moses, and who had

led Israel through the wilderness were not the ones ordained to rule the world to come – that world is to be ruled by the pre-eminent man, the Son of God. The proof of this had been set out for them a thousand years previously: *'But one testified in a certain place, saying: "What is man that you are mindful of him, or the son of man that you care for him? You made him a little lower than the angels, you have crowned him with glory and honour, and set him over the works of your hands. You have put all things in subjection under his feet."'* (Heb. 2:6–8 quoting Ps. 8:4–6)

Paul expounds this passage like this. Although all things are to be in subjection to Jesus, this is not yet finished. As he said in 1 Corinthians 15:26-28, the last enemy to be put under his feet is death. This final step in God's plan is not yet seen but what we can see is that Jesus had been made a man, lower than the angels in order that he should die as the saviour of all who believe. Furthermore, we can also see that he has been elevated way above the angels in status, having been crowned with glory and honour.

To say that Jesus was made a little lower than the angels for the suffering of death is important for a number of reasons. Jesus was made like his brothers of dying sinful nature, all descended from Adam. Death had come upon all such because *'as in Adam all die.'* The angels are not of Adam's race, nor can they die. It was Adam who brought sin into the world through disobedience. God's 'very good' creation was marred. *'Through one man sin entered into the world, and death through sin.'* (Rom 5:12) Reconciliation was immediately offered by our Creator through the promise to raise up the seed of the woman who would, in the fullness of time, destroy sin through a life of perfect obedience and faithfulness to God.

The scribes and Pharisees scoffed at Jesus because they saw him as a man from despised Galilee and had him crucified as a common criminal; condemned as a blasphemer on the authority of the High Priest and Sanhedrin and executed by Pilate. Even so, they had seen that he had been raised from the dead, and that there were many witnesses to his being alive again. They had also seen that through him miracles of healing were continually being done. But all this was contrary to their interests, so they blindly did their utmost to stamp out Jesus' followers. Even the well-known arch-zealot, Saul of Tarsus, had gone over to Jesus and became one of the persecuted instead of the vicious persecutor he once was. Our nature can be very stubborn, prone to justifying itself rather than accepting correction. The evidence for Jesus' death and resurrection has always been overwhelming and vitally important. Little did they realise that they were representatives of the seed of the serpent whom Jesus, as the seed of the woman would destroy.

The captain of their salvation

'For it was fitting for Him, for whom are all things and by whom are all things, in bringing many sons to glory, to make the captain of their salvation perfect through sufferings.' (Heb 2:10) The salvation theme is mentioned five more times in this letter, for example:

- In Hebrews 1:14 *'The heirs of salvation'*

- Hebrews 2:3 *'a great salvation'*

- Hebrews 5:9 *'Eternal salvation'*

- Hebrews 6:9 *'Things which accompany salvation'*

- Hebrews 9:27–28 is the sixth and upbeat occasion: *'Just as people are destined to die once, and after that to face judgment, so Christ was sacrificed once to take away the sins of many and he will appear a second time, not to bear sin, but to bring salvation to those who are waiting for him.'* (NIV)

Just as Jesus had been raised to glory and honour, so many others who are called sons of God would also be crowned. Jesus was a descendant of Adam and like all Adam's seed, subject to the curse. He suffered it and also suffered death. But the point is that he suffered so that by the grace of God he might taste death for everyone.

Because Jesus fulfilled the Law to perfection, something which no other descendant of Adam could do or has done, it would not have been just for him to remain in the grave. Salvation comes to those who believe that Jesus died for their sins and that he rose again for their forgiveness. Such a belief is demonstrated by being baptised into Jesus' death and like Jesus rising again to a new life. Through him all their misdemeanours are wiped out.

All this was foreseen in the Old Testament and came plainly to light with Jesus. As Peter explained to Cornelius and his household, God announced the good news of peace through Jesus Christ that he is Lord of all. He went about doing good and healing all by the power of God. Peter went on to say that he had witnessed the execution of Jesus and also Jesus' resurrection on the third day, something seen by other witnesses chosen by God. All the prophets say that everyone who believes in him receives forgiveness of sins through his name. This is that great salvation mentioned in Hebrews 2:3, which, after listening to Peter's teaching, Cornelius and his household believed and were baptised, God having already baptised them with the Holy Spirit.

Thus, they were included with those described as 'everyone' in Romans 1:16: The gospel *'is the power of God to salvation for everyone who believes, for the Jew first and also for the Greek.'*

This *'great salvation'* did not come through the Law, nor did the baptism of the Holy Spirit. As Paul argued very firmly in the letter to the Galatians. Paraphrasing Galatians 3:3 onward, Paul asserts that they were not given the spirit of God enabling them to do miracles when they were under the Law. It was not given because of their works under the Law, but because they put their faith in Jesus Christ. Having had the wonderful experience of possessing the spirit, how could they possibly think of trying to justify themselves by going back to the Law?

Of course not. No man can make himself just before God. It is God who gives us righteousness through faith in Jesus.

The captain bringing many sons to glory

Returning to Hebrews 2:10–11: *'For it was fitting for Him, for whom are all things and by whom are all things, in bringing many sons to glory, to make the captain of their salvation perfect through sufferings. For both He who sanctifies and those who are being sanctified are all of one, for which reason He is not ashamed to call them brethren…'*

All God's sons and daughters follow the same pattern, first the natural then the spiritual. First as sin-cursed descendants of Adam, then raised to a new life, a new creation. Jesus is the forerunner on that path and we must follow. So far, we have been transferred from being *'in Adam'* to being *'In Christ'*. Christ is our leader as well as the author of our salvation. He has been changed to spirit nature. But at his coming, it will be our turn to be changed in a twinkling of an eye. All of which Paul spells out very clearly in 1 Corinthians 15.

So now Paul wants to impress upon the Hebrews the fact that they and the Lord Jesus Christ are all brothers and uses three references from the Old Testament to prove it, saying: *'I will declare your name to my brethren, in the midst of the assembly I will sing praises to you.'* (Heb 2:12) This quotation comes from the Messianic Psalm 22. It begins: *'My God, My God, why have you forsaken me?',* words uttered by Jesus from the cross.

Paul makes two points by referring to this Psalm. Firstly, that Jesus claimed to have brothers and secondly, it is a Psalm that vividly expresses Jesus' suffering. (Again, notice how Paul gives no clue as to the source of the reference, expecting it to be known to his readers!)

To reinforce the case that Jesus is leading many believers to become children of God and so be saved, Paul makes two quotations from Isaiah 8:17–18. But they are only fragments from the text. The context must have been well known but also accepted as Messianic, otherwise the two fragments would prove nothing.

'I will put my trust in him. And again: Here I am and the children whom God has given me.' (Heb. 2:13) The context of the fragments is significant. The peril Paul's readers were in was a fear of being out of step with the majority and this is the lesson of the context of the two Isaiah fragments.

Here is the context of the two fragments which are to be found in Isaiah 8:11–18):

> *'For the LORD spoke thus to me with a strong hand, and instructed me that I should not walk in the way of this people, saying: "Do not say, 'A conspiracy,' Concerning all that this people call a conspiracy, Nor be afraid of their threats, nor be troubled. The LORD of hosts, Him you shall hallow; Let Him be your fear, and let Him be your dread. He will be as a sanctuary, but a stone of stumbling and a rock of offence to both the houses of Israel, as a trap and a snare to the inhabitants of Jerusalem. And many among them shall stumble; They shall fall and be broken, Be snared and taken." Bind up the testimony, seal the law among my disciples. And I will wait on the LORD, who hides His face from the house of Jacob;* **And I will hope in Him. Here am I and the children whom the LORD has given me!** *We are for signs and wonders in Israel from the LORD of hosts, who dwells in Mount Zion.'* (Isa. 8:11-18)

So much better...

Jesus used this passage from Isaiah to show that it was about himself, although in its preliminary fulfilment *'the children God had given me'* is a reference to Isaiah and his two sons who were to be signs in Israel. They were types of Jesus and his brothers. *'Here I am'* alludes to Isaiah when he volunteered to be God's messenger after he had been given a vision of the glory of the Lord Jesus. *'I saw the Lord sitting upon a throne, high and lifted up; and the train of his robe filled the temple. Above him stood the seraphim. Each had six wings: with two he covered his face, and with two he covered his feet, and with two he flew. And one called to another and said: "Holy, holy, holy is the LORD of hosts; the whole earth is full of his glory!'* (Isa. 6:1-3)

John comments on this in his Gospel: *'But although He had done so many signs before them, they did not believe in Him, that the word of Isaiah the prophet might be fulfilled, which he spoke: "Lord, who has believed our report? And to whom has the arm of the LORD been revealed?" Therefore they could not believe, because Isaiah said again: "He has blinded their eyes and hardened their hearts, Lest they should see with their eyes, Lest they should understand with their hearts and turn, So that I should heal them." These things Isaiah said when he saw His glory and spoke of Him. Nevertheless even among the rulers many believed in Him, but because of the Pharisees they did not confess Him, lest they should be put out of the synagogue; for they loved the praise of men more than the praise of God.'* (John 12:37-43)

So those two fragments turn out to be highly relevant to the Hebrew brothers and sisters – whatever you do, do not follow the crowd. They are heading for destruction. Trust in God as Isaiah did and as Jesus did. Look at Jesus now – seated at the right hand of the Father in glory. He has been raised to the highest glory and honour. You are the children God has given him and are his brothers. Are you going to fall away because you prefer the short-term glory of man to the future glory, honour and immortality promised by God? Did not Isaiah warn against blindness and hardness of heart?

Hebrews 2:14-16 moves to the next step in the exposition, for these words teach a principle of great importance for all generations of believers.

> *'Inasmuch then as the children have partaken of flesh and blood, He Himself likewise shared in the same, that through death He might destroy him who had the power of death, that is, the devil, and release those who through fear of death were all their lifetime subject to bondage. For indeed He does not give aid to angels, but He does give aid to the seed of Abraham.'* (Heb. 2:14–16)

The first part of verse 14 is well understood. Jesus was born as a descendant of Adam and Eve. He had the same nature as us and was subject to the curse like us. But this point is strongly emphasised: *'Inasmuch then as the children have partaken of flesh and blood, He Himself likewise shared in the same…'* The emphasis is made like this: *'he himself likewise.'* Any one of those words would have sufficed to say that Jesus' nature was the same as ours.

The next sentence can seem rather difficult, if not illogical, to a mind confused by false teachers believing the devil to be a non-human opponent of God who seeks to frustrate His plan of salvation. We read: *'that through death he might destroy him who had the power of death, that is, the devil.'* How could Jesus' death destroy this supposedly powerful adversary? Scripture provides the truth of the matter and we must begin with Genesis 3:15. This is about God putting enmity between the serpent and the woman and between their seeds or descendants. The devil is identified in Revelation as *'the dragon, that serpent of old, who is the Devil and Satan.'* (Rev. 20:2)

We are familiar with the fact that 'devil' is a word that comes from the Greek without being translated – a transliteration. The meaning is 'slanderer', or 'liar'. Sometimes the word is translated in the New Testament and sometimes not according to the translators' view of the context. One instance where the word is not translated occurs in John 8:44. Here we have Jesus speaking to Jews, some of whom had previously believed in him. Yet as he spoke, they became so angry with him that they picked up stones to stone him. In his conversation with them Jesus refers to the devil and the children of Abraham, both subjects mentioned in the verses we are considering in Hebrews.

Jesus' teaching in John 8

Jesus said that if they kept his teaching and obeyed it, they were indeed his disciples. Then they would know the truth which would make them free. Hebrews said that Jesus would '... *release those who through fear of death were all their lifetime subject to bondage.'* (Heb. 2:15) Jesus of course meant freedom from the curse of sin and death brought about by the lies of the serpent. The Jews either got the wrong end of the stick or were deliberately obtuse. So, they retorted that they were Abraham's descendants, never having been in bondage to anyone. So, why should they need to be set free? They had apparently forgotten their history of slavery in Egypt, Babylon and the present Roman oppression.

They were growing increasingly indignant, and what Jesus said next implied that they were indeed sinners. He said; *'if you commit sin you are a slave of sin.'* Inasmuch as they were slaves, they were not children of Abraham because a slave is not part of the family. So, although they were descendants of Abraham they were not part of the family unless the son of Abraham set them free. In other words, if they stopped being slaves to sin by believing in the son then they really would be freed from slavery to sin. They could become genuine children of Abraham and children of God by being united in Jesus. Then they would really be part of the family and participants of the promises made to Abraham and his seed. But, what chance was there of that when in fact they were out to kill the seed of Abraham?

These were certainly not the seed of Abraham referred to in Hebrews 2:16, those that Jesus died to help. Or again, just as

Abraham *'believed God, and it was accounted to him for righteousness, therefore know that only those who are of faith are the sons of Abraham.'* (Gal 3:6–7)

Again, Romans chapter 9: *'But it is not that the word of God has taken no effect. For they are not all Israel who are of Israel, nor are they all children because they are the seed of Abraham; but, "In Isaac shall your seed be called"'* (Rom. 9:6–7)

Returning to Jesus' confrontation, by now, Jesus was faced by really angry men, but he continued fearlessly to speak the truth. Defiantly, they asserted: *"'Abraham is our father." Jesus said to them, "If you were Abraham's children, you would do the works of Abraham. But now you seek to kill Me, a Man who has told you the truth which I heard from God…You do the deeds of your father."'* (John 8:39-41)

Now they cast aspersions on Jesus' birth. *'We are not illegitimate children.'* they said. From a human point of view Jesus' birth appeared to have been irregular. Jesus' conception was from on high by the Holy Spirit, but only Mary knew this to begin with. There were no witnesses to the annunciation, nobody else was present when Gabriel told her the good news. Later Joseph was told in a dream and Elizabeth also, was aware of the truth about Jesus' conception. But it was about thirty years later that the voice spoke from heaven to make the public announcement that he was the Son of God. John the Baptist had called Jesus the Lamb of God; this was followed by the voice from heaven declaring *'This is my son whom I love.'* This was later attested to by the miracles, wonders and signs which God did by Jesus. These failed to convince the Jews as this account in John 8 shows. So they boldly said: *'We have one Father— God.'*

Where did this confident assertion come from? From Moses, who was told to say to Pharaoh: *'Israel is My son, My firstborn… if you refuse to let him go, indeed I will kill your son, your firstborn.'* (Ex. 4:22–23)

Jesus could well have had in mind Deuteronomy 32 when he said to them: *'If God were your Father, you would love Me, for I proceeded forth and came from God; nor have I come of Myself, but He sent Me...'* (John 8:42) The word of God in Deuteronomy 32 is forthright in confirming Jesus' words. It was obvious that Jesus was sent from God. He proclaimed the word of the LORD (Deut. 32:3) and the miracles, wonders and signs which God did through him abundantly testified to the fact. Moses demonstrated long before that not only had they rejected God's son but had rejected God Himself. For all that God had done for His people they proved to be a foolish and unwise people who abandoned the God who had made them and rejected the Rock their saviour. (Deut. 32:6,15)

How apposite these words are in this confrontation with Jesus. Had his opponents remembered the context, they should have been chagrined. But they were in no mood to heed the evidence of the word of God, and so the scene comes to its climax. Jesus said: *'The reason you do not understand me is because you cannot.'* No doubt Jesus was alluding to Isaiah 6:10 where the prophet was told that these people would be made blind and deaf in case they understood and were healed. So Jesus accused them: *'You are of your father the devil, and the desires of your father you want to do. He was a murderer from the beginning, and does not stand in the truth, because there is no truth in him. When he speaks a lie, he speaks from his own resources, for he is a liar and the father of it.'* (John 8:44)

Here Jesus has defined the nature of the seed of *'the ancient serpent, the devil and Satan.'* The devil the slanderer of God; the liar; and Satan the adversary. Jesus continued: *'But because I tell the truth, you do not believe me.'* God had taught Adam the truth, but he did not believe it and opted to follow the serpent's lies. So Jesus said to the Jews: *'Which of you convicts Me of sin? And if I tell the truth, why do you not believe Me?   He who is of God hears God's words; therefore you do not hear, because you are not of God.'* (vv. 45–46)

So, by comparing Jesus' teaching in John 8 with Hebrews we learn that Jesus' true brothers are drawn out of all nations to become descendants of Abraham by belief in the Gospel of Salvation. They try to put to death the nature inherited from Adam. They rise from the waters of baptism to a new life in which their sins are forgiven, or to put it another scriptural way, they are given righteousness by God. They have ceased to be the seed of the serpent or devil; ceased to be his followers and have given their allegiance to God and to Christ. They walk in the steps of their father, the father of the faithful, that is, Abraham. This is what is meant by 'aid' in Hebrews 2:16: *'For indeed he does not give aid to angels, but he does give aid to the seed of Abraham.'*

The serpent or devil or liar holds the power of death over the natural seed of Adam. Those who are led by the serpent perish. But those who are led by the seed of the woman have life. They are the true seed of Abraham, people of faith. Not that they will never die, but that they will be saved from death by resurrection and will receive the gift of immortality. Thus, the Scriptures speak of their death as a sleep from which they will awake. Jesus confounded the Sadducees by quoting Moses: *'I am the God of Abraham, the God of Isaac, and the God of Jacob   He is not the God of the dead, but the God of the living. You are therefore greatly mistaken.'* (Mark 12:26–27)

Jesus has destroyed the power of the devil in himself and for those who follow him. The devil no longer holds them in bondage to sin and death. They are no longer fearful of death because they know it is but a sleep, nor are they in bondage to sin because through Jesus, they have access to forgiveness. As the grave could not hold Jesus, so it cannot hold his faithful followers: *'We were buried with Him through baptism into death, that just as Christ was raised from the dead by the glory of the Father, even so we also should walk in newness of life. For if we have been united together in the likeness of His death, certainly we also shall be in the likeness of His resurrection.'* (Rom. 6:4–5)

Jesus a merciful and faithful High Priest

Now another important step is introduced for the first time in this letter. It concerns the High Priest who was the leader of the people. His role was to be the mediator between God and Israel. So Paul introduces Jesus as High Priest by reiterating the point made in verse 2:14 that he had to be made like his brothers in every way. Through this experience he knew what it was like to bear Adam's nature, to understand its weaknesses and trials. It meant that he could be a sympathetic intercessor between his brothers and his and their Father.

Clearly, this arrangement has been made by God for our comfort and encouragement. It is not that God needs an intercessor since as our Creator, He knows us inside out, even knowing our thoughts before we have had them, knowing us from before the foundation of the world. The inference is that God our Father has added this great reassurance for our sakes, that we might understand His profound desire to save us. By this we learn to appreciate the wonderful lovingkindness of our Father, the greatest and most moving expression of which is in the gift of His son.

It is ironic that the Jewish elite made a show of reverence for Moses at the time of this letter's writing, yet when Moses was alive their forefathers treated him just as they had Jesus. As Stephen said: '... *our fathers would not obey, but rejected...Make us gods to go before us; as for this Moses who brought us out of the land of Egypt, we do not know what has become of him.*' (Acts 7:39-40) Exodus records that very soon after the crossing of the Red Sea the Children of Israel became so angry with Moses *that 'Moses cried out to the LORD, saying, "What shall I do with this people? They are almost ready to stone me!"'* (Ex. 17:4) We have already seen in John 8 that the Jews were ready to stone Jesus, a threat that occurred more than once (John 10:31).

Jesus exposed the Jews for what they were, vain hypocrites, making a great show of holiness. Yes, they occupied Moses' seat,

Jesus said, so do what they say but do not be guided by what they do. Jesus then gave a withering account of their behaviour with a list of seven woes concluding with *'Serpents, brood of vipers! How can you escape the condemnation of hell? Therefore, indeed, I send you prophets, wise men, and scribes: some of them you will kill and crucify, and some of them you will scourge in your synagogues and persecute from city to city, that on you may come all the righteous blood shed on the earth… Assuredly, I say to you, all these things will come upon this generation.'* (Matt. 23:33–36)

Moses as a type of Jesus was also a merciful intercessor, even offering his own life to save Israel from destruction. He had, of course, suffered temptation, but was not without sin. The Law given through him could not save Israel from sin and death. Moses, however, was not the High Priest; Aaron was, and the successors to Aaron were strictly specified in the Law.

Under that Law Jesus was debarred from becoming a High Priest and yet Paul wrote that he had to have experienced human nature in order to be a merciful and faithful High Priest. The scribes and Pharisees would have rejected such an appointment as an outrageous violation of the Law. Jesus' appointment as High Priest is dealt with later in the letter (see the chapter headed 'Jesus the compassionate High Priest' beginning on page 58).

Those men who opposed Jesus and thrust him aside as they had Moses are typical of the majority of mankind. They were not literally serpents, but their thinking was crooked like the serpent. They were clever men, but for all that, they did not understand the truth any more than the serpent did, for all his craftiness. They were examples of those described by John in these words: *'… he who does not believe God has made Him a liar, because he has not believed the testimony that God has given of His Son.'* (1 John 5:10)

They were fulfilling the prophecy which spoke of enmity between the seed of the serpent and Jesus, the seed of the woman. As

John points out: *'In this the children of God and the children of the devil are manifest: Whoever does not practice righteousness is not of God...'* (1 John 3:10)

'He who sins is of the devil, for the devil has sinned from the beginning. For this purpose the Son of God was manifested, that He might destroy the works of the devil.' (1 John 3:8)   Sin, or unbelief, is the work of the devil, but as it is, Jesus has appeared once for all at the end of the ages to put away sin by the sacrifice of himself. (Heb. 9:26)

3 CHRIST GREATER THAN MOSES

AN EXPOSITION OF HEBREWS CHAPTER 3

Paul's purpose in writing this letter was to set the revered Moses on one side because Jesus is so much superior in every way. Moses had interceded for Israel, he had led them out of Egypt with great signs and wonders; he had received from God living words to pass on to Israel and yet as Hebrews 3 shows, most of them died in the wilderness because of unbelief. Above all God spoke with him as with a friend face to face. So, although Moses was not a High Priest because God had appointed Aaron to that role, he was above the High Priest in that all God's communication with Israel was through Moses. The last chapter of Deuteronomy describes the greatness of Moses, but even so, Jesus is superior in every way.

Now much of the rest of the letter will demonstrate why Jesus is such a superior intercessor. If the recipients of the letter could really grasp that, then what would be the point of going back to the Law of Moses, even if they were under pressure from Jewish zealots to do so. But the irony of the matter was that Israel persistently rejected Moses in his day and for long after. Now here were Jewish brothers and sisters who had heeded the gospel and been baptised into Christ but were now at risk of being subverted by the religious and political zealots of their day. These zealots had rejected Moses, but meticulously followed their own man-made traditions, and worse still, had rejected Jesus and put him to death. This was such a great risk that most of the epistles include warnings about it.

Consider Jesus

'Therefore, holy brethren, partakers of the heavenly calling, consider the Apostle and High Priest of our confession, Christ Jesus.' (Heb. 3:1) We notice the courteous way Paul addresses them, followed by an exhortation to think deeply about Jesus the

High Priest. This is the only reference to Jesus as an apostle. But that was exactly what he was. He was sent to speak the words God had commanded him to speak. Jesus spoke thus of himself: *'And this is eternal life, that they may know you, the only true God, and Jesus Christ whom you have sent.'* (John 17:3) The last phrase defines the character of an apostle – one sent. Jesus was the supreme apostle, far greater than the great Moses.

The Hebrews had at some time previously, confessed to their faith in Jesus Christ and had been baptised into him, but were considering reverting to Moses as their leader. In the incident in which Miriam and Aaron criticised Moses concerning his Cushite wife, God said that whereas He usually spoke to His prophets in visions and dreams, it was not so with Moses. God said Moses was faithful in all His house and that He spoke with him face to face, in plain language, not in dark sayings. He even saw the form of the LORD. (Num. 12:6–8)

Moses was glorious indeed but even so, not as glorious as Jesus! It was Jesus about whom Moses wrote stern words which were quoted to the Jewish Council by Stephen at his defence. In summary, those words spoke of God sending a prophet like Moses, and the importance of listening to what he said. Hence, the vital exhortation to consider Jesus.

Jesus; the builder of God's house

But now Paul brings forward a new line of evidence in which he compares Moses and Jesus. Jesus was faithful to Him who appointed Him, as Moses also was faithful in all His house. Speaking of Jesus he writes: *'For this One has been counted worthy of more glory than Moses, inasmuch as He who built the house has more honour than the house'. (Heb. 3:3)*

This allusion to the covenant God made with David was most pointed. It was this that led people to expect the Messiah, the one they hoped would restore Israel's greatness as the foremost of the nations. That promise said that there would come one who was greater than David as well as greater than Moses. This one was to be not only David's son but God's son. This one would be the builder of God's house and God would establish the throne of his kingdom forever. (2 Sam. 7:13–14) Zechariah foretold that he should build the house of the LORD bear the glory and rule upon His throne. (Zech. 6:12)

Jesus is still building that house for God's name. Truly an honourable and awe-inspiring responsibility foreshadowed in the work of Solomon in building the Temple. But Solomon admitted that God does not dwell in houses built by men's hands. Entrance into God's house or family is by being born of God through the word of truth (James 1:18). His children are given the surname of their Father and through baptism become God's children. No longer are they children of Adam but children of God. To this day, it has only been a remnant of Israel who have been conscious of their awe-inspiring surname. As Isaiah 43:7 says: *'Everyone who is called by My name, Whom I have created for My glory; I have formed him, yes, I have made him.'*

We ought to be very conscious of the surname we bear because the implications are profound and must influence our attitude and behaviour in every way. The name becomes a very powerful exhortation. Hence Paul addresses his brothers in the faith as holy, having shared the privilege of the calling of God from heaven.

The wonder of it all is expressed by Peter:

> *'But you are a chosen generation, a royal priesthood, a holy nation, His own special people, that you may proclaim the praises of Him who called you out of darkness into His marvellous light; who once were not a people but are now the people of God, who had not obtained mercy but now have obtained mercy.'* (1 Pet. 2:9–10)

In this passage Peter changes the metaphor to speak of Jesus as a living stone in God's house, which he calls a spiritual house. You are also living stones and being used in the building of the house. The metaphor changes in other contexts where Jesus is called the foundation stone, headstone of the corner, and again the believers are called living stones. So, we are seen to be not only the fabric of God's house, but the occupants as well. No wonder Paul gives such a solemn exhortation to Timothy: *'if I delay, you may know how one ought to behave in the household of God, which is the church of the living God, a pillar and buttress of the truth.'* (1 Tim. 3:15 ESV) We are dwelling with God in His house and must also be supports to His truth. Keep it, know it, teach it and live it.

But notice also how significant John 14 becomes in the light of these things. Jesus said: *'If anyone loves Me, he will keep My word; and My Father will love him, and We will come to him and make Our home with him.'* (John 14:23)

Building the Tabernacle

Every house needs someone to build it and the builder of this house is God. Moses faithfully built the house according to the plans given him by God and it was called the Tabernacle of Testimony or the tent of Testimony (Num. 10:11; 9:15). It testified to the true house to be built by God in due course. So, Paul compares Moses and Christ. Moses, as a servant testified about things which were to be spoken later. For example, he was commanded to say to Israel: *"Let them make me a sanctuary, that I may dwell in their midst."*

The tabernacle was made, and the LORD was metaphorically enthroned between the cherubim. But Israel never saw him! The throne, the mercy seat, was hidden in the Holy of Holies. The tabernacle was beyond a fence of linen forming the outer court. The Israelites were camped all round it but were nonetheless, kept at arm's length. Even Moses was not allowed into the throne room. Only Aaron, and even then, very briefly on the Day of Atonement.

The tabernacle and the Law nonetheless testified of many things which were to be made plain later. The contrast between these laws and Christ is great. Jesus has gone into the real presence of God in the heavens: *'For Christ has not entered the holy places made with hands, which are copies of the true, but into heaven itself, now to appear in the presence of God for us;'* (Heb. 9:24) An astonishing allegory is taught by Paul when he wrote that in the great mercy of God: *'He has raised us up together with Christ and made us sit together in the heavenly places in Christ Jesus.'* (Eph. 2:4–6) In other words Christ's brothers and sisters, who are part of his body, are seated in the antitypical most holy.

All this is so unlike the relationship which Israel had with God under the leadership of the servant, Moses. The arm's length relationship is replaced by a close fatherly one. We are to call Him Abba. We may speak to Him, and we have a High Priest to intercede for us. He is not a mortal man who does not know one Israelite from another, but a brother who understands us perfectly – *'but Christ as a Son over His own house, whose house we are if we hold fast the confidence and the rejoicing of the hope firm to the end.'* (Heb.3:6)

The appeal to those Judaisers of the First Century should have been irresistible. So much better in every way are the things which have been brought to pass through Christ.

Exhortation from Psalm 95
Whilst we are not in danger of joining the Jewish zealots, there are many other dangers that could draw us away from our position of extreme privilege in Christ. So, a vital exhortation comes next. The writer quotes half of Psalm 95, a Psalm of David. Notice in passing that Hebrews says that the words are those of the Holy Spirit, a reminder that all Scripture is of God.

It is important to read the whole Psalm because the sequence of thoughts is the same as in the letter to the Hebrews. It seeks to impress Israel with the extreme privilege of their position before God.

(Ps. 95:1–7) The Psalm begins by encouraging exuberant and joyful songs of praise to the rock of our salvation. It recognises that God is so great and the Creator of all things and makes this appeal: *'Oh come, let us worship and bow down; Let us kneel before the LORD our Maker. For He is our God, and we are the people of His pasture, And the sheep of His hand...'* (Ps 95:6-7)

So Israel, consider this, says the Holy Spirit; think of the greatness of God and yet, wonder of wonders, He is our God, and we are the people of His pasture, and the sheep of His hand. Even so they strayed away from Him; hence the relevance to the argument being put forward in Hebrews. So, the Psalm continues:

> *'... Today, if you hear his voice, do not harden your hearts, as at Meribah, as on the day at Massah in the wilderness, when your fathers put me to the test and put me to the proof, though they had seen my work. For forty years I loathed that generation and said, "They are a people who go astray in their heart, and they have not known my ways." Therefore, I swore in my wrath, "They shall not enter my rest."'* (Ps. 95:7–11 ESV)

We are familiar with Israel's behaviour in the wilderness, but notice the very strong language used by the Holy Spirit. They had been taken out of Egypt with amazing signs and wonders: they had walked through the sea; they had been terrified at the mount of God; they had been fed and watered; their clothing had not worn out etc. As if this were nothing, they still doubted that God would bring them into the land. They tested Him to see whether they could trust Him or not. But God declared, *'They are a people who go astray in their heart, and they have not known my ways.'* They had not thought it important to attend diligently to these things. Consequently, terrible words were spoken by the Holy Spirit: - *'For forty years I loathed that generation.'*

To be loathed by the Almighty is an appalling thought. And yet the Jews remain as unbelieving as ever and the Gentiles to whom the Gospel of Salvation has gone forth are no better. Only a remnant has sought to know God and to walk in His ways because they have taken the trouble to place His words into their hearts. It is a matter of great sorrow to us that some of our own children do not heed the word of God and some have forsaken it, as if these vital lessons had never been learned. But let us not despair for them because the point of this quotation is to say that there is still time to repent. 'Today' still exists and the opportunity to repent remains.

> *'Take care, brothers, lest there be in any of you an evil, unbelieving heart, leading you to fall away from the living God. But exhort one another every day, as long as it is called "today", that none of you may be hardened by the deceitfulness of sin. For we have come to share in Christ, if indeed we hold our original confidence firm to the end.'* (Heb. 3:12–14 ESV)

4 DO NOT HARDEN YOUR HEARTS

AN EXPOSITION OF HEBREWS CHAPTER 4

Hebrews Chapter 3 explained that those who believe God and obey Him become His children and then dwell with Him in His house, with Jesus as the head of the household. The next point is that Israel, whom God called out of Egypt, never reached the Land of Promise because of their failure to trust God. God tested them to see whether or not they had faith. They failed, dying in the wilderness and so never entered into the promised rest. The lesson for the Hebrew recipients of the letter was clear. Israel had a great leader in Moses, and they rebelled against him. Now the prophet like unto Moses had come, who was a much greater prophet than Moses. Were they going to rebel against him too, and let themselves be persuaded to go back to the Law of Moses and forsake the far better way in Christ?

The promised rest

So, chapter 4 explains that the rest promised to the faithful is still available to this day. Psalm 95 is quoted to prove the point. Although Joshua led the next generation of Israel into the land, that did not constitute the rest that was promised. They never finished the conquest of the land promised to Abraham and so many of the inhabitants of the land continued to live in it and they seriously corrupted Israel. Much of Israel's history shows how troubled their lives were and how often they were under heathen domination. Furthermore, the promises were made to Abraham and Jesus alone; only those who shared the faith of Abraham were counted as his children. Only those united with Christ through belief and baptism are counted as the singular seed of Abraham. Chapter 4:9 explains what that rest meant: *'for he who has entered his rest has himself also ceased from his works as God did from his.'*

When Jesus was accused of working on the Sabbath he answered: *'My Father has been working until now, and I have been working.'* (John 5:17)... even on the Sabbath!

What work is God engaged in? The 'very good' creation of Genesis 1 had been spoiled by sin, and so God is working on a new creation. Notice how often the Gospel of John mentions work and works; it far exceeds that of any other New Testament book. This is to be expected because that Gospel opens with an account of creation; not the Genesis1 creation but the new creation which God is working to create in and by and through our Lord Jesus. The beginning referred to is the beginning of Jesus' ministry and his disciples were with him at that beginning. Hence, Jesus said to his disciples: *'But when the Helper comes, whom I will send to you from the Father, the Spirit of truth, who proceeds from the Father, He will testify of Me. And you also will bear witness, because you have been with me from the beginning.'* (John 15:26–27)

The promised rest still in the future

It follows that the Sabbath of rest of this new creation is still in the future. *'For if Joshua had given them rest, then He would not afterward have spoken of another day.'* (Heb. 4:8) Evidently, Israel's entry into Canaan to establish the Kingdom of God is a type of something else. *'Since therefore it remains that some must enter it, and those to whom it was first preached did not enter because of disobedience, again He designates a certain day, saying in David, "Today," after such a long time, as it has been said: "Today, if you will hear his voice, do not harden your hearts."'* (Heb. 4:6–7)

When we examine the context of these words of David, we see that the subject is creation and salvation. The Psalm invites people to sing for joy to the LORD, the rock of our salvation. It goes on to describe His creation and exhorts us to kneel before our Creator. Such are the people of His pasture, the flock He cares for as a shepherd. The rest of the Psalm shows that the flock that came out of Egypt hardened their hearts against the shepherd, failing to understand the LORD and were barred from entering into that rest.

It is a picture of a persistently wayward flock, always going astray. So, this letter to the Hebrews is addressed to yet another generation of the same flock, a flock who were in danger of falling into unbelief, about which Moses said: *'You have seen all that the LORD did before your eyes in the land of Egypt... Yet the LORD has not given you a heart to perceive and eyes to see and ears to hear, to this very day.'* (Deut. 29:2–4) Isaiah reiterated these sentiments (Isa. 6:9–10).

This generation, to whom the letter appeals, had also seen the wonders of God's work through Jesus Christ and were on the point of hardening their hearts. So, the urgent exhortation follows: *'Let us therefore be diligent to enter that rest, lest anyone fall according to the same example of disobedience.'* (Heb. 4:11)

Of course, these urgent exhortations are every bit as imperative to us who have been grafted into the Israel olive tree. The obvious danger facing us is to lose our faith in the promises of God and turn back to the world.

God at work

We will look at Scriptures from elsewhere which speak of God's work. For example, Philippians 2:12–13: *'...work out your own salvation with fear and trembling; for it is God who works in you both to will and to do for His good pleasure.'* We see that there are two workers mentioned here; first we are to work out our salvation, but secondly, and amazingly, God is working in us to accomplish His will and pleasure. For our part we work in fear and trembling.

We need to be careful about the meaning of the words 'fear and trembling'. The first letter of John says: *'There is no fear in love; but perfect love casts out fear, because fear involves torment. But he who fears has not been made perfect in love.'* (1Jn 4:18)

Evidently, something is wrong if we are fearful of our heavenly Father in whose house we dwell as children. We love the Father because we are deeply conscious of the love He has shown us in calling us to be His children. This ought to produce in us the strong emotion of being awestruck. We are in the presence of this infinitely great being who has not only taken notice of us but has shown us such love. And yet our awe-inspiring Father wants us to think of Him as a child does his father and call Him Abba, Father. W.E.Vine in his *Expository Dictionary of New Testament Words* says that:

> 'Abba is the word framed by the lips of infants, and betokens unreasoning trust. Father expresses the intelligent apprehension of the relationship. The two together express the love and intelligent confidence of the child.'

What of the trembling? We can tremble with terror, but that cannot be the meaning here because it implies that we have not understood the love of God. But we can also tremble with excitement, and this must be the sense of this passage. We are in a state of awe and wonder in the presence of our Father. If we always felt like that, we would do all we could to work harmoniously with God. In other words, says John: *'We love Him because He first loved us.'* (1John 4:19)

We return to the main point about God at work. In the first chapter of Philippians Paul expresses his thankfulness to God for the fellowship he has with the Philippians and says that he is confident that God who began His work in them will complete it.

The one who began the work is God. He is the one who chooses and calls those He wishes to work upon. *'For we are His workmanship, created in Christ Jesus for good works, which God prepared beforehand that we should walk in them.'* (Eph. 2:10)

The context of this verse is of God calling certain ones to come close to Him and join His family. They have believed and been baptized into Christ and have become members of the body created in Christ Jesus. Later he explains that God can do far more than we could possibly imagine through His power that is at work in us (Eph. 3:20).

God's power at work in us

We ask, how does God's power work in us? One way is through the word of God as is explained by Paul in the letter to the Thessalonians. He thanked God because the Thessalonian brothers and sisters accepted his teaching as the very words of God, and that word was working in them (1Thess. 2:13). Through the word we are under the influence of God and Jesus. Ephesians exhorts us to imitate God just as Israel were exhorted to emulate God because of His kindness to them. The effect will be that we grow to show forth or manifest the character of God just as Jesus did.

God also works in us by answering prayer. An example from the letter to the Hebrews is:

> '*Now may the God of peace .... make you complete in every good work to do His will, working in you what is well pleasing in His sight through Jesus Christ, to whom be glory forever and ever. Amen.*' (Heb. 13:20–21)

Another example of prayer is found in Ephesians 1:16–20:

> '*I do not cease to give thanks for you, making mention of you in my prayers: that the God of our Lord Jesus Christ, the Father of glory, may give to you the spirit of wisdom and revelation in the knowledge of Him, the eyes of your understanding being enlightened; that you may know what is the hope of His calling, what are the riches of the glory of His inheritance in the saints, and what is the exceeding greatness of His power toward us who*

believe, according to the working of His mighty power which He worked in Christ when He raised Him from the dead and seated Him at His right hand.'

We conclude with this instruction from Jesus when he was asked *'What must we do to work the works of God?'* Jesus' concise answer was: *'believe in the one He has sent.'* (John 6:28–29) This is the essence of the letter to the Hebrews. Do not forsake Jesus for Moses; believe Jesus.

The living and active word of God

Now comes a stern reminder:

'For the word of God is living and powerful, and sharper than any two-edged sword, piercing even to the division of soul and spirit, and of joints and marrow, and is a discerner of the thoughts and intents of the heart. And there is no creature hidden from His sight, but all things are naked and open to the eyes of Him to whom we must give account.' (Heb. 4: 12–13)

The gospel was preached to those who fell in the wilderness (Heb. 4:2) but it was of no value to them because they did not believe it. The good news for them was that God had prepared rest from their toils in Egypt in the land promised to Abraham and his descendants. They were doubtful, and so sent spies to inspect it; they were told that it was a good land yet were fearful of the well defended cities. In short, they did not believe that God could give it to them, in spite of their astonishing deliverance from Egypt. They failed to trust in God who had brought them thus far. Yet that word was living and active and would have given them rest if they had shown the same faith as Abraham had done.

God made Abraham the father of the circumcised i.e., the natural descendants through Isaac and Jacob. It was some of them who protested to Jesus when he offered to make them free: *'We are Abraham's descendants, and have never been in bondage to anyone.'* (John 8:33) This was a tragically common error of the thinking of the Jews. But the crucial point is that it was not enough to be circumcised physically. Those counted as Abraham's children must walk in the footsteps of the faith that Abraham had before he was circumcised.

The faith of Abraham

Abraham's faith was seen in Genesis 15:4–6: *'And behold, the word of the LORD came to him, saying, "This one shall not be your heir, but one who will come from your own body shall be your heir." Then He brought him outside and said, "Look now toward heaven, and count the stars if you are able to number them." And He said to him, "So shall your descendants be." And he believed in the LORD, and He accounted it to him for righteousness.'* It was a fine demonstration of faith in God's promises. It entailed belief in the miraculous, a miracle huge in its scope. But this is what God requires of all who seek salvation. We must believe in what is humanly impossible, i.e. resurrection from the dead; eternal life; the possession of the kingdom of God on earth even though the world is at present occupied by many nations. Abraham believed all of that. All of it miraculous.

That generation which fell in the wilderness witnessed colossal miracles which could only be by the hand of God. Despite that evidence, they could not muster enough trust to take the land He had promised to give them.

The exhortation is that the kind of faith God looks for has been shown in the example of Abraham. God discerns the thoughts and intentions of the heart and knows whether we possess such faith. He also knows all our failings and weaknesses. Hence the point of the next step in the argument.

Jesus the compassionate High Priest

An essential element of faith is the confidence that our Father is very merciful and invites us to speak to Him to ask for help.

'Seeing then that we have a great High Priest who has passed through the heavens, Jesus the Son of God, let us hold fast our confession. For we do not have a High Priest who cannot sympathize with our weaknesses, but was in all points tempted as we are, yet without sin. Let us therefore come boldly to the throne of grace, that we may obtain mercy and find grace to help in time of need.'
(Heb. 4:14-16)

What a comfort these words are to all who believe them. But consider what they would have meant to our first century brothers and sisters who were tempted to fall away to Judaism. Jesus the Son of God, not a servant as Moses was, is seated in the very presence of God himself. Once upon a time they confessed to a belief in him and were baptized into him. By comparison, the High Priest serving in the temple in Jerusalem was a frail mortal man; acquisitive, exploiting the ordinary worshippers, politically motivated and determined not lose his station in the state.

In stark contrast, Jesus as the great High Priest knew what they were going through and really understood their frailty. He was sympathetic to their trials, because he had been a mortal man himself, and so had experienced such weakness and knew what temptation was. He knew that they were going through a tough and testing time. The remedy was, draw near to the throne of grace, confident in the knowledge that you will be understood and you will be shown mercy and help in your time of need. What more reassurance could they wish for?

5 JESUS THE COMPASSIONATE HIGH PRIEST

AN EXPOSITION OF HEBREWS CHAPTER 5

So now Paul has opened a new line of evidence in demonstrating the superiority of Jesus over Moses and the Law. Chapter 4 finished with the exhortation to hold fast to the hope we profess because we have a marvellous High Priest, who from personal experience understands us and can sympathize with us in our weaknesses. He is the bridge between us and Almighty God. Chapter 5 explains that Jesus, as our High Priest, has been appointed by the Almighty to enable us to approach Him boldly.

No wonder Paul describes Him as our gracious God, for He has given us this access to Himself through Jesus. Jesus was not like Aaron and the High Priests who succeeded him, who were variable in character, were sinners and not always sympathetic towards those they were to represent to God. Indeed, Jesus suffered from the terrible injustice of the high priesthood which flouted the law to bring about his death. None of the High Priests of the New Testament were even descendants of Aaron; far from being appointed in accordance with the Law of Moses, they were appointed by the Roman administration. They were Hasmoneans, of the Maccabean family of the tribe of Judah. They did not become High Priests upon the death of the previous High Priest, but were dismissed and appointed on the whim of the Roman Governor. Annas was the father of the family, Caiaphas was his son-in-law.

The point is that the High Priest could not appoint himself. The honour of representing Israel to God and God to Israel was by God's appointment.:

> 'And no man takes this honour to himself, but he who is called by God, just as Aaron was. So also Christ did not glorify Himself to become High Priest, but it was He who

said to Him: "You are my Son, today I have begotten you.' (Heb. 5:4–5 quoted from Ps.2:7)

'Christ did not exalt himself'

Jesus did not begin to carry out his ministry to the house of Israel until He was appointed by God. As he arose from the waters of baptism, God declared publicly via *'a voice* [that] *came from heaven which said, 'You are My beloved Son; in You I am well pleased.'* (Luke 3:22) It is also wonderful to remember that we did not exalt ourselves to become sons and daughters of God and brothers and sisters of Jesus Christ. We were called by God to be born again through the waters of baptism. We were also born of the spirit in the sense that through the word of God, we came to understand and believe the Gospel of Salvation. Provided that we endure faithfully to the end, then like him, we shall be raised to glory and immortality.

We return to Paul's reasoning. When God said: *'You are my Son, today I have begotten you'*, he was reiterating what He had said one thousand years previously in Psalm 2:7. It is instructive to follow Paul's teaching in the synagogue in Antioch in Pisidia where he was telling the Jews about Jesus. He taught that what God had said through David in the second Psalm: *'You are my son, today I have begotten you'* had come to pass in their day and he was a witness to it. God had raised Jesus. The inference of this is that Jesus became God's son in the complete sense when he was raised to the divine nature. In the same way, we are being created by God as members of the new creation which will, on completion, raise us to the divine nature. Jesus is the first born of that new creation, or the first fruits, as Paul writes in 1 Corinthians 15.

Paul continued his address in Antioch by saying that having raised Jesus from the dead never again to die, God had fulfilled what He had said in His promise to David: *'I will give you the sure blessings promised to David.'* It was this great promise which enabled David to rest in hope of his own resurrection to life eternal, to see his son rule from his throne over God's kingdom. Paul continued by quoting Psalm 16:10: *'Nor will You allow Your Holy One to see corruption.'* He then continued by expounding the importance of this fact. He said: *'Therefore let it be known to you, brethren, that through this Man is preached to you the forgiveness of sins; and by Him everyone who believes is justified from all things from which you could not be justified by the law of Moses.'* (Acts 13:38–39) This is the point; Jesus, raised by his Father from the dead to divine nature, and declared to be the Son of God, fulfilled the covenants to Abraham and David. The covenant with Abraham provided forgiveness of sins through faith, something the Law of Moses could not do. The covenant with David gave him the hope of resurrection. It showed that God's promise to give David a son who would both build the house for God and reign on David's throne, was progressing in accordance with the good counsel of His will.

Another point arises from *'You are my son'*. Remember that God took the Levites to be the firstborn of Israel in place of Reuben and in place of every firstborn male born in Israel. They are called by God, 'mine' (Num. 8:17). The appointment of the High Priest was further narrowed down to Aaron and his descendants. Aaron was also the firstborn son of Amram. It was the tribe of Levi who rallied to Moses at the terrible event of the golden calf and was henceforth separated to be the priestly tribe. Previously, the priesthood was usually the role taken by the first-born son. When the Law of Moses became obsolete, God appointed His firstborn and only begotten son to be the High Priest, although he was not of the tribe of Levi, but of Judah. So, the reasoning continues with another reference from the Psalms.

Jesus appointed a High Priest by God

Psalm 110 has the title 'A Psalm of David' and makes the point plainly that Jesus had been raised not only to the priesthood but to immortality as well. *'As He also says in another place: "You are a priest forever according to the order of Melchizedek."'* (Heb. 5:6)

Then comes the amazing evidence from the Psalm: *'The LORD said to my Lord, "Sit at My right hand, Till I make Your enemies Your footstool."'* (Ps. 110:1)   This is the point made in Hebrews 4:14. The resurrected Jesus, the great High Priest, has gone through the heavens, Jesus the Son of God and son of David. Even so, the LORD will send His son back to the earth to rule from Zion. *'The LORD shall send the rod of Your strength out of Zion. Rule in the midst of Your enemies!'* (Ps. 110:2)   Also, as Psalm 2:6 says: *'Yet I have set my King on My holy hill of Zion.'*

In chapter 6 the exposition continues with a further reference to Psalm 110: *'The LORD has sworn and will not relent...'* (Ps. 110:4) These words are extremely emphatic and refer to yet another one of those promises which God confirmed with an oath. Also confirmed in this way are the vital promises to David and to Abraham. (Gen. 22:16, Ps. 89:3) This one is about Jesus' appointment as a priest forever. Where then does that leave the Law of Moses? Where did it leave the advocates for returning to that Law?

Psalm 110 covers a great span in time. It speaks of Melchizedek who lived about one thousand years before David. It speaks of our Lord Jesus, two thousand years after David, but from the viewpoint of today, some three thousand years after the Psalm was written. Part of it was fulfilled about two thousand years ago and the rest remains to be fulfilled.

The exposition continues with a summary of Jesus' life on earth. The facts of Jesus' suffering were well known to the readers. Much of his suffering was at the hands of those who were then disturbing the peace in the ecclesias. Jesus, while sharing our nature as a mortal man, suffered from being attacked frequently by his enemies. He knew that they would put him to death to be rid of him once and for all. But Jesus believed that God would save him from death to fulfil His many promises. So, although he suffered so much, offering prayers with loud cries and tears to his Father, the last occasion being in Gethsemane, his obedience and trust were vindicated. He was raised to immortality and incorruptibility; he was made perfect. Even though he was the Son of God he learned obedience through his experiences. Thus he opened the way to eternal salvation for all who follow his example. Now this man is at the right hand of God in the heavens, interceding for those who are attempting to follow his example.

Exhortation

The exposition in Hebrews chapter 5 is interrupted here by exhortation. He speaks of Melchizedek…

> *'… of whom we have much to say, and hard to explain, since you have become dull of hearing. For though by this time you ought to be teachers, you need someone to teach you again the first principles of the oracles of God; and you have come to need milk and not solid food. For everyone who partakes only of milk is unskilled in the word of righteousness, for he is a babe. But solid food belongs to those who are of full age, that is, those who by reason of use have their senses exercised to discern both good and evil.'* (Heb. 5:11–14)

Spiritual growth is expected of all God's children and Paul exhorts us to make the effort to grow in understanding. We can use an example from ordinary life. Parents are eager to see their children well educated, to grow in knowledge and wisdom so that they will be equipped for life. It would be disappointing if the child remained undisciplined, ignorant, lazy and unmotivated. Our Heavenly Father sees a lazy attitude towards the teaching of His word as disappointing.

'It is able to make us wise unto salvation'.

To neglect the reading of it implies a lack of respect and enthusiasm for salvation so graciously offered to us by our Heavenly Father. Obviously, we can become dull of hearing; we can forget and so need to revise or be taught again. Obviously, we ought to try to be skilled in the word of righteousness and not remain as a child, but grow to maturity. Constant practice is the training which enables us to discern between good and evil. It does not matter how long we have been in the Truth, we must not allow ourselves to relax in our meditations on the word of God and then responding to its influence. Paul continues this exhortation in chapter 6.

6 DO NOT REVERT TO CHILDHOOD

AN EXPOSITION OF HEBREWS CHAPTER 6

Paul continues the exhortation begun in Hebrews 5 with these words:

> 'Therefore, leaving the discussion of the elementary principles of Christ, let us go on to perfection, not laying again the foundation of repentance from dead works and of faith toward God, of the doctrine of baptisms, of laying on of hands, of resurrection of the dead, and of eternal judgment. And this we will do if God permits.' (Heb. 6:1–3)

It is one thing to be childish when one is a child but absurd for an adult to revert to childishness. *'Dead works'* were the rituals of the law which could not save them from death. Works without faith can save no one. The metaphor concerns building and foundations which must be well and truly laid if they are to be built upon. They are not interfered with after the superstructure is in construction. In Galatians 4:1-9, Paul points out that in going back to Judaism, they were regressing to childhood and in need of the supervision of adults. They were seemingly unaware that their Father expected them to be ready for the responsibilities and privileges of grown up sons.

> 'Now I say that the heir, as long as he is a child, does not differ at all from a slave, though he is master of all, but is under guardians and stewards until the time appointed by the father. Even so we, when we were children, were in bondage under the elements of the world'. (Gal. 4:1–3)

The elements of the world refer to Judaism. So Paul shows that at the time appointed by God, Jesus was brought into the world, born of Mary and born under the Law. His role was to redeem or free those who were under the Law, treating them as grown-ups rather than children in need of supervision. The fact was that when they were under the control of a guardian, they were no different from a slave – they had to do as they were told. But they had grown past that juvenile phase and were now treated as sons and heirs. The Father is God, so now they were sons of God (Gal. 4:7).

Paul asked; 'Surely you do not want to go back to childhood with all the loss of freedom it brought with it?' Desiring again to be in bondage is just what the Hebrews were doing in reverting to the childish elementary principles of the Law of Moses, principles which taught about Christ but only in a shadowy way. Israel showed their immaturity after the Exodus by desiring to go back to bondage in Egypt where they had good things to eat. But just as they had seen the majesty and mighty works of their God in the Exodus, so they had now seen Jesus and his mighty works. They had seen the substance rather than the shadow. Were they going to abandon salvation through Christ and the freedom from the Law for the *'worthless elementary principles of the world, whose slaves you want to be once more?'* (Gal. 4:9 ESV) It was a solemn exhortation.

Christ was no shadow; he was the body itself, the substance. In fact, far from being a shadow, he was the light of the world. He said in John 12:46: *'I have come as a light into the world, that whoever believes in Me should not abide in darkness.'* The shadow is dark, the reality is the light of Christ. No wonder the exhortation is severe.

However, in principle, the lesson is applicable to all. We have been instructed in the elementary teaching of the Gospel of Salvation, the foundation which led us to repentance. We declared that we believed it and showed our belief by being baptised – our first act of obedience. As far as we are concerned dead works means this:

'For when you were slaves of sin, you were free in regard to righteousness. What fruit did you have then in the things of which you are now ashamed? For the end of those things is death. But now having been set free from sin, and having become slaves of God, you have your fruit to holiness, and the end, everlasting life'. (Rom. 6:20–23)

A stern warning

Returning to Hebrews chapter 6, a severe warning gives the reader a shock:

'For it is impossible for those who were once enlightened, and have tasted the heavenly gift, and have become partakers of the Holy Spirit, and have tasted the good word of God and the powers of the age to come, if they fall away, to renew them again to repentance, since they crucify again for themselves the Son of God, and put Him to an open shame.' (Heb. 6:4–6)

The words *'it is impossible'* are worrying and we need to study the meaning carefully, because we too have been enlightened just as the Hebrews had been. God has opened our hearts to know the Gospel of Salvation. But have we tasted the heavenly gift? It refers to the Holy Spirit which was given to the apostles at Pentecost, to others such as Cornelius, and those upon whom the apostles laid hands. Peter shows however that 'the heavenly gift' is more than this and includes *'the pure milk of the word.'* He wrote:

'… having been born again, not of corruptible seed but incorruptible, through the word of God which lives and abides forever,… this is the word which by the gospel was preached to you… desire the pure milk of the word, that you may grow thereby, if indeed you have tasted that the Lord is gracious.' (1 Peter 1:23–2:3)

We have tasted that the Lord is gracious. He has offered to save us on condition that we believe in Him. He has given us forgiveness of sins, or to put it another way, He has given us righteousness. He gave us Jesus who was delivered over to death for our sins and was raised to life for our justification. All of this is entirely due to the graciousness of the Almighty; in no way did we deserve such a gift. We have not received the Holy Spirit in the sense of being empowered to expound the word of God or to carry out miracles, but we do have the word which He moved His servants to write and which is so powerful that it will save us from perishing and give us eternal life. All who have been baptised into Christ should have experienced the change that comes upon them by being led by the spirit of God. In Romans 8, Paul explains the power of the spirit word to influence our behaviour. The effect of that influence is described in the familiar words of Galatians 5:22–25: *'But the fruit of the Spirit is love, joy, peace, longsuffering, kindness, goodness, faithfulness, gentleness, self-control. Against such there is no law. And those who are Christ's have crucified the flesh with its passions and desires. If we live in the Spirit, let us also walk in the Spirit.'*

Paul's appeal is to think most carefully. They had once been enlightened; they had tasted the heavenly gift, shared in the Holy Spirit and had tasted the goodness of the word of God and the powers of the age to come. To experience all these wonderful things and then fall away is likened to trampling on the Son of God. Is repentance impossible for those who fall away? Is it impossible then to be brought back to repentance? We all know of brothers and sisters who have fallen away. Some have simply swamped the Truth with the affairs of this world. Others have deliberately declared that they have lost their faith in God's word and yet others rebel against His precepts. Others have disobeyed the Truth but later repented of their disobedience and come back like the prodigal son to their Father.

Leaving and returning

The fact is that the Scriptures are full of such cases. It is only too easy to grow slack; to be seduced by the distractions of this world and slowly fall away, or to be mentally lazy and not apply the mind to the Word and be led away. The notorious example is Solomon who had been wonderfully blessed with the gift of wisdom. Even so he fell away: *'The LORD was angry with Solomon, because his heart had turned away from the LORD, the God of Israel, who had appeared to him twice and had commanded him concerning this thing, that he should not go after other gods. But he did not keep what the LORD commanded.'* (1 Kings 11:9–10 ESV) Evidently Solomon did not repent, for it is reasonable to suppose that if he had, he would have destroyed the detestable high places which he had built for his idolatrous wives, women he should not have married in the first place. He built shrines on the hill east of Jerusalem to Ashtoreth the goddess of the Sidonians and Molech the detestable god of the Ammonites that he followed. These awful things were actually facing the Temple which he had built for the LORD God of Israel. It was to Molech that children were offered in the fire, acts of almost unbelievable superstition. It was not until the days of Josiah that those detestable high places were destroyed (2 Kings 23:13).

It is a woeful example of human weakness that Solomon had forgotten his prayer to God when dedicating the house which he had faithfully built:

> *'When the heavens are shut up and there is no rain because they have sinned against You, when they pray toward this place and confess Your name, and turn from their sin because You afflict them, then hear in heaven, and forgive the sin of Your servants, Your people Israel, that You may teach them the good way in which they should walk; and send rain on Your land which You have given to Your people as an inheritance.'* (2 Chron. 6:26–27)

On the other hand, there is the case of Manasseh. He led Judah and Jerusalem to do more evil than the nations the LORD had destroyed before the Israelites. The LORD brought the Assyrians against him and he was taken captive to Babylon, led with a hook in his nose.   It is astonishing to read:

> 'Now when he was in affliction, he implored the LORD his God, and humbled himself greatly before the God of his fathers, and prayed to Him; and He received his entreaty, heard his supplication, and brought him back to Jerusalem into his kingdom. Then Manasseh knew that the LORD was God.' (2 Chron. 33:12)

Asa was taught: 'The LORD is with you while you are with Him. If you seek Him, He will be found by you; but if you forsake Him, He will forsake you.' (2 Chron. 15:2)

These cases show that repentance is possible if we entreat the LORD as did Manasseh. On the other hand, if we forsake him until the end of our days then He will forsake us. This lesson is taught thoroughly in Ezekiel 18:21–25.

Scripture does not contradict itself, so further investigation is necessary to find the answer. To begin with, we note these words of Jesus: 'If I had not done among them the works which no one else did, they would have no sin; but now they have seen and also hated both me and My Father.' (John 15:24). Again he said: 'But if I cast out demons by the Spirit of God, surely the kingdom of God has come upon you.' (Matt. 12:28)   God did these wonders through Jesus to attest to the truth that he was His son. 'Therefore I say to you, every sin and blasphemy will be forgiven men, but the blasphemy against the Spirit will not be forgiven men. Anyone who speaks a word against the Son of Man, it will be forgiven him; but whoever speaks against the Holy Spirit, it will not be forgiven him, either in this age or in the age to come.' (Matt. 12:31–32)

So, to have seen the God-given evidence that He was working through His son in miracles of healing and yet ascribe the power of God to Beelzebub was blasphemy against the Holy Spirit. We know that some of the Jewish Christians had been given the gifts of the spirit and used them to teach, to heal and to speak in tongues. Even so, having tasted these powers, some were in effect rejecting the evidence that Jesus was the Son of God by returning to the Law. So, the blasphemy amounts to this; they were joining those who had hated Jesus so much, that nothing but Jesus' death would satisfy them. In doing so, they would subject Jesus again to the shame he had endured during his ministry, his trial and crucifixion as a common criminal. That sentence meant, as Jesus' enemies knew full well, that he was cursed by the law which said *'he who is hanged is accursed of God.'* (Deut. 21:23) No doubt, they imagined that in crucifying Jesus they had ensured that he would be condemned by God as well as themselves.

Hence Hebrews 6:6 says that to follow such a course would in effect crucify the Son of God all over again. This would subject him to public disgrace although he was the one pre-eminent man. Peter addressing the Jewish council said of him: *'Nor is there salvation in any other, for there is no other name under heaven given among men by which we must be saved.'* (Act 4:12)

This, I suggest, is the blasphemy for which repentance was impossible.

God's vineyard, the allegory of the soil
On the face of it the next two verses seem to be disconnected but are actually, very much to the point. *'For the earth which drinks in the rain that often comes upon it, and bears herbs useful for those by whom it is cultivated, receives blessing from God; but if it bears thorns and briers, it is rejected and near to being cursed, whose end is to be burned.'* (Heb 6:7–8)

Isaiah had presented a parable on this subject using the same figure. It illustrated God's careful preparation of His vineyard, planting the best of vines. He waited for the fruits to come, anticipating good grapes, but what a disappointment when it produced wild grapes.

God asked what more could I have done for my vineyard to produce a good harvest? So he decides to destroy the vineyard, laying it waste and allowing briars and thorns to flourish there. The parable ends with an ominous warning saying that the vineyard of the LORD of Hosts is the house of Israel (Isaiah 5:1–7)

The curse upon Adam also resonates here (Gen. 3:17–19). Under this curse, land left to itself will, in the main, produce useless thorns and thistles. Cultivation and toil are essential to produce good fruit to eat. God will water and cause the seeds to sprout into the plants which are being cultivated, but man still has to labour in constant weeding, thinning out, pruning, harvesting etc. It is a self-evident reality which confronts us every time we go into our gardens. If we neglect it for a few weeks, especially in Spring and Summer, the weeds will multiply, and much hard work will be necessary to bring the land back to order. In the allegory, the land represents us. But we are also the labourers. The land has been cursed and left to itself produces sin and death, that is *'if it bears thorns and briers, it is rejected and near to being cursed, whose end is to be burned.'*

This allegory is used in many places in Scripture, for example: *'Who then is Paul, and who is Apollos, but ministers through whom you believed, as the Lord gave to each one? I planted, Apollos watered, but God gave the increase. So then neither he who plants is anything, nor he who waters, but God who gives the increase. Now he who plants and he who waters are one, and each one will receive his own reward according to his own labour. For we are God's fellow workers; you are God's field…'* (1 Cor. 3:5-9) The seed is the Gospel which reminds us of Jesus' parable of the sower.

Again, our gardens teach us that marvel. All our clumsy toiling is nothing compared with the miracle of the growth of seed into plants and fruits of such amazing variety and abundance.

The lesson of the parable of the vineyard in Isaiah 5 was often repeated by the prophets and finally, by Jesus and yet it was ignored. For Jesus too, came to cultivate the LORD'S vineyard. He used the same allegory in the parable of the tenants of the vineyard, a parable recorded in all the synoptic gospels. The tenants refused to give the owner's servants the fruits due to him and worse, abused them. So, He sent his son because surely, they would respect the son. Not so! They killed him.

Jesus asked those listening to the parable what they thought the owner of the vineyard would do when he comes? They said to him, *'He will destroy those wicked men miserably, and lease his vineyard to other vinedressers who will render to him the fruits in their seasons.'* Jesus said to them, *'Have you never read in the Scriptures: "The stone which the builders rejected has become the chief cornerstone. This was the Lord's doing and it is marvellous in our eyes?" Therefore I say to you, the kingdom of God will be taken from you and given to a nation bearing the fruits of it. And whoever falls on this stone will be broken; but on whomever it falls, it will grind him to powder.'* This was a very stern warning and, it is astonishing to read that the chief priests and Pharisees knew that he was talking about them (Matt. 21:42–44)

Strong encouragement

We are not told how those to whom the letter was written responded, but it would not be for want of encouragement.

> *'But, beloved, we are confident of better things concerning you, yes, things that accompany salvation, though we speak in this manner. For God is not unjust to forget your work and labour of love which you have shown toward His name, in that you have ministered to the saints, and do minister. And we desire that each one*

of you show the same diligence to the full assurance of hope until the end, that you do not become sluggish, but imitate those who through faith and patience inherit the promises.' (Heb. 6:9–12)

The letter goes on to discuss the promises, but before continuing we notice some important teaching in the four verses we have just read.

- *'Things that accompany salvation.'*

- *'For God is not unjust to forget your work and labour of love.'*

Their work consisted of the services they had shown to the saints, a work carried out because of their love for God. Such service is seen in those who seek and believe the promises of salvation and is real evidence of the sincerity of their faith. The first letter of John teaches that if we love God, then the proof of that love is seen in our love for His children.   On the other hand, lack of love for God is this: *'If anyone loves the world, the love of the Father is not in him. For all that is in the world—the lust of the flesh, the lust of the eyes, and the pride of life—is not of the Father but is of the world.'* (1 John 2:15,16)

So, Paul urges them to maintain their diligence by continuing to show that it is their hope in God which motivates them. He mentions in passing the conviction of those examples of faithful endurance which will be the subject of chapter 11.

Paul does not leave the matter there, but goes on to show why our diligence is encouraged by two facts. Firstly, God notices and does not forget and secondly, God has guaranteed the hope He has promised in an astonishing way.

For Abraham's sake, God swore by Himself

So, the letter goes on in a most persuasive and unexpected way to show how intent God is to encourage His children. He cites Abraham to whom God had made the important promise to give Abraham a son. After a long wait, that promise was eventually fulfilled, but Abraham's faith was further tested when God command him to offer his only son as a sacrifice. Because of his obedience and trust, God swore with an oath to bless Abraham and make his descendants as numerous as the stars in the sky and as the sand on the seashore. But the record in Genesis 22:16 said specifically that *'God swore by Himself.'* Paul observes that God did this because He could swear by no one greater. More than that even, the absolute certainty that the promises would be performed was the fact that God cannot lie. It means that the hope we have in the promises of God are rock solid, immutable, an anchor sure and steadfast, which secures our hope.

The encouragement presented here shows how determined the Almighty Creator is to call us to salvation. Why should He plead with us to be saved? Why should He want to convince us of His offer of salvation by swearing about it with an oath? After all, God is truth and it is impossible for him to lie. The answer is given in Hebrews 6:18 (ESV): '... [that] *we who have fled for refuge might have strong encouragement to hold fast to the hope set before us.'* The same exhortation appeared in verses 11 and 12. *'And we desire that each one of you show the same diligence to the full assurance of hope until the end, that you do not become sluggish, but imitate those who through faith and patience inherit the promises.'*

Paul writes very powerfully about this attitude of mind in 2 Corinthians 5:13–18. Some thought he was out of his mind in his zeal for proclaiming the Gospel, but he was only doing what God had called him to do. This is his answer: - *'For if we are beside ourselves, it is for God; or if we are of sound mind, it is for you. For the love of Christ compels us, because we judge thus: that if One died for all, then all died; and He died for all, that those who live should live no longer for themselves, but for Him who died for them and rose again.'*

So, we are motivated by the love of God and of Christ. If we have really understood the lengths they have gone to, to enable us to be saved, then it compels us to respond in faith and loving service.

Fled for refuge

Notice the allusion to the cities of refuge in verse 18: *'we who have fled for refuge'*. It is sin and death that we are fleeing from, the curse of mortality. Under the Law, the one who had unintentionally killed a person could flee to certain designated cities where they were safe from the avenger of blood. The Law stipulated that they must remain in the city until the death of the High Priest. Hebrews goes on to show that our High Priest will never die! Therefore, we must remain safely in the city of refuge for the rest of our lives. But, if we are so foolish as to leave the city, to leave Christ, in other words leave the Truth, then we must accept the consequences of death at the hand of the avenger of blood. It is tantamount to throwing God's offer of salvation back in his face.

Christ our intercessor

But that is not all. Christ, the one who died that we might have this hope of salvation, has gone into the inner sanctuary, behind the curtain, the place where the High Priest went once a year to obtain forgiveness for all the people. The figure is the Tabernacle, but the reality is heaven itself where Jesus Christ is interceding for us before God, not as a mortal High Priest, but as an ever-living High Priest who knows what it is like to be a mortal human being. This has already been spelt out emphatically in chapters 2 and 4. Jesus has entered on our behalf says Hebrews 6:20, which is an amazing fact, hard for our mortal minds to comprehend.

Jesus is called 'our forerunner'

The sense in which Jesus is our forerunner is of one who has gone ahead, as expounded by Paul in his first letter to Corinth: *'But now Christ is risen from the dead, and has become the firstfruits of those who have fallen asleep.'* (1 Cor. 15:20) The evidence for the resurrection of Jesus is powerful and guarantees the resurrection of all who have had their eyes opened to the Truth as it is in Jesus. Chapter 6 concludes with a new thought that is developed fully in chapter 7. Paul explains that Jesus has become High Priest forever according to the order of Melchizedek.

7 MELCHIZEDEK

AN EXPOSITION OF HEBREWS CHAPTER 7

The letter to the Hebrews was written to persuade Jews not to abandon the Gospel of Salvation in Christ and go back to the Law of Moses. So far, the case made for the superiority of Jesus has been:

- As God's son, he was greater than the prophets

- As God's son, he is greater than the angels

- As God's son, he is greater than God's servant Moses

- His priesthood is greater than that under the Law

- He is greater than Joshua

Now a new line of evidence is presented which is rather surprising. Its strength however is that it has to do with Abraham, the great Jewish patriarch and his association with Melchizedek.

Chapter 6 ended by saying that Jesus had entered the real Most Holy in the heavens and was a priest forever in the order of Melchizedek. Chapter 7 begins by saying that Melchizedek was a priest of the most-high God who met Abraham returning from rescuing Lot after the battle of the four kings against five. Not only was Melchizedek a priest, he was also King of Righteousness and King of Salem, which means King of Peace. Abraham honoured this man by giving him a tenth of the spoil from his battle with the four kings.

In chapter 5 we saw that no man could assume the honour of becoming a High Priest. The appointment was made by God. Just as Aaron and his four sons were appointed by God, so was this man Melchizedek, and even Jesus did not become High Priest without God's appointment. Melchizedek has been the subject of much discussion which arises from Paul's comments about him. Why, for example is he said to be without father or mother? Why did he say that he was without beginning or ending of days? Scriptural references to Melchizedek are few. In fact, there are only three: Genesis 14, Psalm 110 and the letter to the Hebrews and each one was written about 1,000 years apart.

The historical character

This is the Genesis account: Abraham, victorious over the four kings, was himself met outside Jerusalem by two kings. The King of Sodom had travelled across the plain to the north of the Dead Sea and climbed up to Jerusalem where he met Abraham in the Valley of Shaveh, just outside Jerusalem to the south. Much more importantly, King Melchizedek also came out to meet him and blessed him. It implies that Abraham was considered a conquering hero, blessed by God whose victory was cause for celebration: *'And he blessed him and said: "Blessed be Abram of God Most High, Possessor of heaven and earth; and blessed be God Most High, Who has delivered your enemies into your hand."'* (Gen. 14:18–20)

It would seem that the King of Sodom represented the five kings of the plain in negotiating the return of the captives rescued by Abraham. In exchange for the captives, he offered the spoils taken from the cities of the plain. Abraham refused to accept anything from the wicked King of Sodom, saying that he had sworn to the LORD, not to take a thing belonging to them to prevent them claiming that they had made him rich. It was an entirely different matter when the King of Salem, priest of God Most High, came out to meet Abraham with bread and wine. He blessed Abraham and Abraham gave him a tenth of the booty.

The contrast between these two kings is great. On the one hand was the King of Sodom, whose city was soon to be utterly destroyed *'because the outcry against Sodom and Gomorrah is great and their sin is very grave.'* (Gen 18:20) On the other hand was a king declared to be priest of God Most High. So, Abraham refused the gift offered by the wicked king, but his gift to Melchizedek indicates grateful acceptance of the blessing from God through God's appointed priest. Melchizedek provided bread and wine, symbols pregnant with meaning, the sharing of which signified fellowship and reminds us of the sacrifice of Abraham's seed. Abraham would have regarded the sharing of a meal of fellowship as a mark of honour bestowed on him by this representative of the LORD God Most High. Sharing a meal or a feast in Abraham's day and ever since is a celebration of fellowship. That is a brief summary of the historical details concerning Melchizedek.

The Psalmist's comment

A thousand years later, David wrote in Psalm 110: *'The LORD said to my Lord, "Sit at My right hand, Till I make Your enemies Your footstool." The LORD has sworn and will not relent, "You are a priest forever according to the order of Melchizedek."'* (Ps. 110:1,4) The words *'you are a priest forever'* are addressed to Jesus, whereas neither Genesis nor Psalm 110 mentions Melchizedek's ancestry, or say anything about him being ever-living. Why does David make this seemingly tenuous reference to Melchizedek? The opening sentence was in a sense, partly true of Abraham. God did make Abraham's enemies a footstool for his feet when he overcame four powerful kings who had defeated many other nations, besides overwhelming the kings of the five cities of the plain. God had intervened and miraculously delivered them into Abraham's hand. They had been made Abraham's footstool, although he did not sit at God's right hand. That honour was to be given to his seed, but he did take a most energetic role in the conquest.

Although we can see King Melchizedek as a type of the future role of King Jesus, Hebrews is focussed on the priestly type from Psalm 110: *'The LORD has sworn and will not change his mind,*

"You are a priest forever according to the order of Melchizedek.'"
Why was a change of priesthood necessary?

To find the answer, we move forward approximately another 1,000 years to the final mention of Melchizedek. Paul under inspiration expounds the brief facts given in the Old Testament, some of which could easily be overlooked. He refers to Melchizedek's blessing of Abraham. This much we have already discovered from Genesis 14. But now, new exposition emerges. Paul reiterates that Abraham gave a tenth part of all to Melchizedek and tells us that he was named 'King of Righteousness' and also 'King of Salem' which means 'King of Peace.' Isaiah teaches this about Jesus: *'Of the increase of His government and peace there will be no end.'* (Isa 9:7)   We need to remember the meaning of peace, especially in relation to Jesus as the antitypical King of Peace and King of Salem. The meaning is clearly taught in Romans 5 and again the context concerns Abraham: *'Therefore, having been justified by faith, we have peace with God through our Lord Jesus Christ.'* (Rom. 5:1) Jesus is the one through whom God reconciles us to Himself, and with reconciliation comes peace.

Two more features are taught. It is reasoned that since Melchizedek blessed Abraham, he was the greater of the two men. The indisputable principle is that the greater blesses the lesser. This thought is expanded like this; Melchizedek was a man and therefore mortal. He lived long before Abraham's descendent Aaron was born. So, the superiority of Melchizedek is proved by Abraham's respect for him in that he paid tithes to Melchizedek. But an unexpected deduction is drawn from this. In effect Abraham's descendants, the Levites, paid tithes to Melchizedek even though they had not been born. Those descendants themselves became recipients of tithes under the Law and were honoured in this way, but even so were inferior to Melchizedek. By implication therefore, the Law too, was inferior.

As so much is deduced from Melchizedek's blessing of Abraham, it is puzzling to read that Melchizedek also said: *'blessed be God*

Most High, who has delivered your enemies into your hand!' (Gen. 14:20) In no sense could God be said to be the lesser blessed by the greater in this case. Yet the Hebrew word is the same in both instances. The Hebrew word is *barak* and is used many times with reference to God. Strong's Concordance gives its sense as 'to kneel before', implying 'adoration.' *'Bless the LORD O my soul'* is one of many examples where the word means 'thankfulness'. This seems to be the sense when Melchizedek said: *'blessed be God Most High, who has delivered your enemies into your hand!'*

Melchizedek – without father, without mother

Hebrews 7:3 continues with a new fact. Melchizedek was *'without father, without mother, without genealogy, having neither beginning of days nor end of life, but made like the Son of God, remains a priest continually.'* On the face of it, this is a puzzling verse. However, it is important to remember the purpose of this letter which was to warn the Hebrews against leaving the Gospel of Salvation through faith in Jesus for the Law. A comparison is being made between the Law of Moses and the New Covenant. This letter has much to say about that covenant later. The New Covenant made the forgiveness of sins possible. The Law could not. Forgiveness was made possible through faith, not by works. It is demonstrating that the Law had done its work and was now redundant. So, the inadequacies of the Law are demonstrated one by one. Melchizedek and Jesus were not constrained by the Law; Melchizedek, because the Law did not exist in his days and Jesus' ministry, as an everlasting priest, was after the Law had become obsolete.

Under the Law, God commanded that the priests should be descended from Aaron and his sons. Only they were allowed to serve at the altar and within the Tabernacle. Anyone disobeying this command was to be put to death. (Ex. 28; Num. 3:1–3; Ezra 2:61–62.) So, the genealogy of an individual descendant of Aaron had to be proved before he could serve as a priest. On his death, he had to be succeeded according to strict laws concerning descent. Not so with Melchizedek. He was not bound by genealogy, and so his parents were not regarded or recorded; he was priest by direct appointment of God Most High. His birth and death are not recorded either and no descendant succeeded him as priest. He was a priest appointed by God long before the Law was given to Israel. The record simply says that he lived and therefore the things recorded in the history about his relations with Abraham truly occurred. Jesus' appointment as priest occurred after his resurrection to everlasting life. Hence his priestly role would be forever.

Next, we are taught that perfection could not be achieved through the Law. The Law demonstrated how sinful the people were, whereas in Christ, forgiveness of sins is possible through faith in him. Such forgiveness is a gift from God and is frequently referred to as the gift of righteousness. It can never be earned, nor can a person ever claim to be righteous by their own endeavours (Rom. 5:17; Gal. 5:5; Eph. 1:7; Phil. 3:8,9; 2 Tim. 4:7,8; Tit. 3:4-7).

Paul continues: *'Therefore, if perfection were through the Levitical priesthood (for under it the people received the law), what further need was there that another priest should arise according to the order of Melchizedek, and not be called according to the order of Aaron?'* (Heb. 7:11) Perfection was not possible under the Levitical priesthood, and so it was essential that another priest should be appointed. This priest would obviously not be a descendant of Aaron as required by the Law, but would be appointed directly by God most high, just as Melchizedek was.

Forgiveness depends on a better priesthood

But notice this concerning the mortality of Melchizedek; perfection depended upon a better priesthood than that of Aaron, but we can also deduce that it depended on a better priest than Melchizedek. Perfection, sinlessness, or righteousness could not come through Melchizedek. He did not offer himself as a sinless sacrifice, but was as dependent upon the gift of righteousness through faith as all faithful men and women. That principle was established in

Genesis 15:6 in the very next step in the history of Abraham: *'And Abraham believed the* LORD, *and He counted it to him as righteousness.'*

The priesthood instituted by God under the Law of Moses has been demonstrated to be inferior to that of Melchizedek in that Abraham's unborn descendants (he had no son at this time) paid tithes to Melchizedek and received a blessing from him.

The next point in demonstrating the inadequacy of the Law is this: *'For the priesthood being changed, of necessity there is also a change of the law.'* (Heb. 7:12) Jesus has been appointed priest forever; therefore the Law has been made obsolete. The Levitical priesthood had become redundant for it was superseded by a better priesthood. The role of the priesthood was central to Israel, prescribing their conduct in every aspect of their national and personal lives. Changing it was a shock which rocked the foundations of the establishment. Hence the constant attacks upon Jesus' teaching and actions such as his healings on the Sabbath.

The radical nature of the change is further emphasised by this fact: *'For he of whom these things are spoken belongs to another tribe, from which no man has officiated at the altar. For it is evident that our Lord arose from Judah, of which tribe Moses spoke nothing concerning priesthood.'* (Heb. 7:13–14)

The order of Melchizedek

So, what does the order of Melchizedek mean? Surely, it consists of a specific appointment by God which did not depend upon pedigree; hence no record of his birth or death was necessary. His appointment was unique. Jesus is of that order or rank inasmuch as: *'And it is yet far more evident if, in the likeness of Melchizedek, there arises another priest who has come, not according to the law of a fleshly commandment, but according to the power of an endless life.'* (Heb. 7:15–16)

Notice how carefully the legal argument is presented. It is focussed on the Law. The Law was precise about the pedigree of the priest. Melchizedek was a priest long before the Law. Jesus was appointed priest after the Law had become obsolete. Their appointments had nothing to do with any legal requirement in the Law of Moses.

Notice that Jesus has a pedigree of the greatest importance which was completely independent of the Law. He is unique in that his bodily descent was from Abraham and David, but also of God. No other man had such origins. Nor has any other man been raised to everlasting life or appointed by God with an oath to be a priest forever. The fact that another priest was appointed in the order of Melchizedek implies the death of Melchizedek and the need for a successor, one appointed by God with an oath just as Melchizedek had been. Neither appointment had anything to do with the Law of Moses.

The inadequacy of the Law is demonstrated by the fact that it was now useless: *'For on the one hand there is an annulling of the former commandment because of its weakness and unprofitableness, for the law made nothing perfect; on the other hand, there is the bringing in of a better hope, through which we draw near to God.'* (Heb. 7:18–19) The appointment of Jesus in the order of Melchizedek outside the Law had brought about the end of the Law.

It is interesting to note in passing how Paul describes himself before he knew the Lord Jesus. (Phil. 3:5–6) *'circumcised the eighth day, of the stock of Israel, of the tribe of Benjamin, a Hebrew of the Hebrews; concerning the law, a Pharisee; concerning zeal, persecuting the church; concerning the righteousness which is in the law, blameless.'* Blameless, so he thought, but the fact was that *'that law made nothing perfect.'* He continued by saying that all he had achieved through his own effort was of no value. What was of inestimable value was to receive the righteousness given him by God through faith. Any

Hebrew honestly weighing the evidence must have been persuaded not to waiver but to remain wholeheartedly faithful to Christ.

The better hope

What follows in verse 19 is wonderful. *'… for the law made nothing perfect; on the other hand, there is the bringing in of a better hope, through which we draw near to God.'* (Heb. 7:19)

This observation is a considerable understatement. The contrast is tremendous. It is between a law that condemned all to death in spite of all the works it demanded, and a better hope, which enabled forgiveness and everlasting life through faith, not works of law.

Now another legal detail is brought forward. Like Melchizedek, Jesus was appointed by the LORD with an oath. So, again the superiority of the new and better arrangement is emphasised by the importance placed upon it, in that God confirmed it with an oath. This was not the case with the Levitical priesthood. God did this for our sakes as Hebrews has already told us. (Hebrews 6:16-18). All the great promises of God have been thus confirmed. The promises to Abraham: (Gen.22:16; 26:3; Deut.7:8; 13:17; 19:8; 29:13; 31:7; Ps.105:9,10; Jer. 11:5; Mic. 7:20). The promises to Israel: (Deut.28:9); To David: (Ps. 89:35; 132:11; Acts 2:30; Heb.6:13). And the great promise of God concerning himself (Num.14:21).

Further thoughts about Melchizedek and Abraham

- Melchizedek appeared only once to Abraham, but God had appeared to Abraham at Ur and many times afterwards (Acts 7:2; Gen.12:7; 13:14; 15:1; 17:1; 18:1; 22:1).

- God blessed Abraham, repeating the promises and confirming them with an oath without any priestly mediation.

- Abraham himself built altars and offered sacrifices without a priestly mediator.

- Was Abraham a priest? It appears so. In being willing to obey God's command to offer Isaac, he was a type of the Father of our Lord Jesus.

- Abraham interceded for Lot and the cities of the plain.

- Abraham interceded for Abimelech and was declared to be 'a prophet', God's spokesman. (Gen. 20:7)

Abraham was a priest, yet he was blessed by a priest-king appointed by God Most High who was even greater than himself. That priest-king was typical of our Lord Jesus Christ. Therefore, as Melchizedek was declared to be greater than Abraham, surely Jesus as the antitype, is demonstrated to be greater than Abraham. This is a fact with which we are familiar, but it would be an important point to make to Jews hesitating about returning to the Law of Moses. It had already been shown that Jesus is superior to Moses; Moses was a servant in God's household whereas Jesus is the son. Again, David called his greater son Lord, indicating that even though he was David's son, he was greater than David.

The better covenant

So, we now look at the way the argument is developed in urging faithfulness to Christ rather than deserting him for the Law of Moses. It is developed by introducing 'a better covenant' and the contrast is tremendous. It is between a law that condemned all to death in spite of the works it required, and a better covenant which provided forgiveness and everlasting life through faith. Concerning the Law, Jeremiah was instructed to say to the men of Judah and Jerusalem: 'Cursed is the man who does not obey the words of the covenant which I commanded your fathers when I brought them out of Egypt.' (Jer. 11:3–4) Clearly that covenant was the Law of Moses. God continued, obey my voice and do what I command you, then you will be my people and I will be your God. I will also bring upon you the oath I made with your fathers to give you the land flowing with milk and honey (paraphrasing Jer.11:4–8).

By contrast Paul now draws attention to a new and better covenant to which Jesus stood surety. We will look at this New Covenant under chapter 8, where it is quoted verbatim from Jeremiah.

The weakness of the law

Yet another legal point is brought forward to demonstrate the weakness of the Law. Due to their mortality, there had to be a continuous succession of priests under the Law. The priests inevitably had to be changed following the death of the priest. Not so in Jesus' case. His priesthood is everlasting because he is everlasting. So his priesthood is not subject to change. Paul spells out the great advantages of this priest. He is always there for those who want to come to God through him, to intercede with his Father in whatever their need may be. (This point is tremendously emphasised in Romans 8:31, where God himself is said to be for us.) Our priest is harmless, having no evil thoughts towards us. This contrasts with the High Priest and the priests who were intent upon destroying Jesus.

This chapter has previously referred to Jesus as 'priest' but it changes here to 'High Priest.' The earlier exposition has Psalm 110 in mind, which speaks of a priest of the order of Melchizedek rather than High Priest. Now the comparison is with the High Priests under the Law, inferior though they were, nonetheless they foreshadowed Jesus.

So, the exposition continues by pointing out the differences between those High Priests and Jesus. Unlike them, Jesus was undefiled, was sinless and now separated from them as far as the heavens are above the earth. He does not need to offer daily sacrifices for sins for himself and the people. He made one supreme sacrifice in offering himself for the sins of the people, an offering effective for ever. All of this is underlined by the fact that the Law appointed as High Priests men who bore all the weaknesses of Adam's nature. Jesus, appointed with the oath, was now perfected by being raised to the divine nature.

It is interesting to see how the profound difference between Jesus and the mortal priesthood was foreseen by Malachi. In rebuking the Levitical priests, he exposed their weaknesses by comparing them with Jesus, the messenger of the LORD:

> *'My covenant was with him, one of life and peace, and I gave them to him that he might fear Me; so he feared Me and was reverent before My name. The law of truth was in his mouth, and injustice was not found on his lips. He walked with Me in peace and equity, and turned many away from iniquity. For the lips of a priest should keep knowledge, and people should seek the law from his mouth; For he is the messenger of the LORD of hosts. But you have departed from the way; You have caused many to stumble at the law.'* (Mal 2:5–8)

Digression: The partial blindness of Israel

Why were the Jews unable to understand the work of God through Jesus? Why did they stumble over that rock which is Christ? Even the twelve apostles stumbled. When Jesus asked them: *'Why are you discussing the fact that you have no bread? Do you not yet perceive or understand? Are your hearts hardened? Having eyes do you not see, and having ears do you not hear?'* (Mark 8:17–18 ESV) Jesus was alluding to Isaiah 6 and asked, had they forgotten the miracles of feeding the five thousand and the four thousand?

Paul, no doubt deeply conscious of his error as Saul of Tarsus, answers our questions in his letters. For example in 2 Corinthians 3, he says that God had made him a minister of the 'New Covenant' (v6), which was announced through Jeremiah (Jeremiah 31:31–34) and twice quoted in the letter to the Hebrews. The marvellous feature of this New Covenant was the forgiveness of sins, not based on works but upon knowing the LORD. The Greek verb *ginosko* is used here and translated 'know'. It means having a real knowledge and understanding of a person. This is contrasted with a slavish keeping of the law. Paul said that the letter kills. By this he meant the letter of the Law. The law condemned man and made him aware or conscious of his sins. Even so, that Law was glorious because it was God given and its laws were therefore just. It taught them that God had separated them from the nations around them to be holy because He is holy. They had been chosen by God to be His special treasure, a people who would show the nations the blessings of having the LORD as their God.

> *'Behold, I have taught you statutes and judgments, even as the LORD my God commanded me, that ye should do so in the land whither ye go to possess it. Keep therefore and do them; for this is your wisdom and your understanding in the sight of the nations, which shall hear all these statutes, and say, Surely this great nation is a wise and understanding people. For what nation is there so great, who hath God so nigh unto them, as the LORD our God is in all things that we call upon him for? And what nation is there so great, that hath statutes and judgments so righteous as all this law, which I set before you this day?'* (Deut. 4:5–8)

That law was written on stone and was a ministry which showed the Jews that they deserved death, along with all Adam's descendants. When Moses came down from the presence of God with the stone tablets, his face shone with a brilliance which made it necessary to place a veil over his face. Gradually that brilliance faded. The fading signified the fact that, glorious though that law was, it would fade away to give way to a New Covenant which was so much better than the old (2 Cor. 3:9–11). The glory of the New Covenant would be so much more glorious that it would eclipse the old.

Nobody could keep the Old Covenant; consequently everyone was condemned to death by it. Even Christ was cursed under that law by the nature of his death in being crucified. But, under the New Covenant, God would write His law, not on stone tablets, but on their hearts. Then they would all know the LORD from the least to the greatest, and He would forgive their iniquity, no more to be remembered. But for now, that veil remains in place, says Paul. When the Old Testament is read, its meaning is veiled from their sight. The veil was lifted by Christ so that those who believed in him could see.

The Jewish people in general, who had so cruelly rejected Jesus, remained blind, and to this day, when Moses is read, a veil lies on their heart. Their blindness and deafness, that spirit of stupor, (Rom.11:8) self-evidently remains to this very day. Some of them do try to uphold the law by meticulous observance, not understanding that salvation is by grace. As Paul wrote: *'but Israel, pursuing the law of righteousness, has not attained to the law of righteousness.'* (Rom. 9:31) Israel, looking for a righteousness derived from Law, nonetheless failed to do what that Law required. In other words, they thought that they could be righteous through their own efforts and therefore be worthy of recompense. The law of righteousness meant that righteousness would be given to the man who had faith in God rather than in his own abilities. As Paul explains:

> *'Why? Because they did not seek it by faith, but as it were, by the works of the law. For they stumbled at that stumbling stone. As it is written: "Behold, I lay in Zion a stumbling stone and a rock of offence, and whoever believes on him will not be put to shame."'* (Rom. 9:32–33)

God speaking through Isaiah explains why this is so and again we quote Isaiah: *'Go, and tell this people: "Keep on hearing, but do not understand; keep on seeing, but do not perceive." 'Make the heart of this people dull, and their ears heavy, and shut their eyes;*

lest they see with their eyes, and hear with their ears, and understand with their heart, and return and be healed.' (Isa. 6:9–10) Jesus quoted these words when his disciples asked why he spoke to the people in parables (Matt.13:13–15). Paul also referred to the same passage when trying to teach the gospel to some Jews in Rome. Some believed but others did not (Acts 28:23–27).

Because they were so stubbornly rebellious, Paul wrote in Romans 1:24: *'God gave them up to uncleanness... For this reason God gave them up to vile passions… Even as they did not like to retain God in their knowledge, God gave them over to a debased mind.'* (Rom 1:24–28) Nonetheless, God has promised: *'The deliverer will come out of Zion, and he will turn away ungodliness from Jacob.'* (Rom. 11:26)

The restoration of Israel

It is wonderful to read in Ezekiel 36 what God will do with Israel in the future. Speaking of the day of the LORD He says:

> *"'I will sanctify My great name, which has been profaned among the nations, which you have profaned in their midst; and the nations shall know that I am the LORD,"* *says the Lord GOD, "when I am hallowed in you before their eyes. For I will take you from among the nations, gather you out of all countries, and bring you into your own land. Then I will sprinkle clean water on you, and you shall be clean; I will cleanse you from all your filthiness and from all your idols.* [Now notice the language of the New Covenant:] *'I will give you a new heart and put a new spirit within you; I will take the heart of stone out of your flesh and give you a heart of flesh.'"*

Then the words of the New Covenant are reiterated:

> *'I will put My Spirit within you and cause you to walk in My statutes, and you will keep My judgments and do*

them. Then you shall dwell in the land that I gave to your fathers; you shall be My people, and I will be your God.' (Eze. 36:23–28)

The same heart-warming message is taught by Paul in Romans 11:25–29. Indeed, concerning the gospel they were enemies from whom Paul had suffered so much persecution. Those to whom Paul wrote were also suffering from attempts by the Jews to undermine their faith. Nonetheless, Israel are beloved for the sake of the fathers and Isaiah expresses the mind of God in heart-warming terms:

> *'For Zion's sake I will not hold My peace, and for Jerusalem's sake I will not rest, until her righteousness goes forth as brightness, and her salvation as a lamp that burns. The Gentiles shall see your righteousness, and all kings your glory. You shall be called by a new name, which the mouth of the LORD will name. You shall also be a crown of glory in the hand of the LORD, And a royal diadem In the hand of your God.'* (Isa 62:1-3)

Then Israel will be a wise and understanding people, conforming to God's will expressed in Deuteronomy 4:5–8. It will surely come to pass. Of course, we wonder when the day will come, but it will be when God has completed the calling of the Gentiles. We must wait patiently knowing that God's promises are irrevocable and that we have had the immense privilege of having been included in that fullness.

8 THE SUPERIORITY OF CHRIST'S MEDIATION

AN EXPOSITION OF HEBREWS 8

The main point is that Jesus, the High Priest, is serving in the tabernacle erected by God in the heavens. He is seated there at the right hand of the throne of majesty. This is called the throne of grace in chapter 4:16. Under the Law, the High Priest entered the Most Holy Place once a year and was not allowed to dally there. Jesus, however, is not only seated at the right hand of God but remains there until he is sent to judge the world with righteousness.

There is a stark contrast here when we think of the state of affairs in Judah contemporary with the writing of this letter. Annas and his family had led the nation to reject Jesus and crucify him. They were acting as High Priests in the colossal temple restored by Herod. How could the Hebrews contemplate deserting Jesus to go back to a system of worship led by such evil men, focussed on a temple built by the man who had tried to destroy Jesus as a child?

The Law was only a shadow
Next, the ministry of Jesus is contrasted with the Law. The first point is that Jesus did not qualify under the Law to serve as a priest. However, that Law was about things on earth not things in heaven. The Law was only a copy and a shadow of the real tabernacle in the heavens. When Moses was instructed to make the Tabernacle, God said *'See that you make everything according to the pattern I showed you on the mountain.'* Jesus was the substance, the real High Priest and the sacrifice for sins to which the Law had pointed forward. The Law was put in charge of God's people until the seed promised to Eve, Abraham and David had come. Christ had come and was now High Priest. He had presented the perfect sacrifice, without blemish; not a mere animal but himself. Paul points out that if Jesus was on earth, he would not be a priest. But he was the priest appointed by God to serve

in the real Tabernacle; the inference is that the sons of Aaron were in no respect qualified to serve as priests in the real Tabernacle.

Jesus is mediator of a better covenant

'But now he has obtained a more excellent ministry, inasmuch as He is also Mediator of a better covenant, which was established on better promises.' (Heb. 8:6)

Paul teaches what *'Mediator of a better covenant'* entailed:

> *'For there is one God and one mediator between God and men, the man Christ Jesus, who gave Himself a ransom for all, to be testified in due time.'* (1 Tim. 2:5–6)

That due time had come. Paul's ministry was to testify to the Gentiles this good news, i.e., that salvation was offered to both Jews and Gentiles on the basis of faith in the promises of God. God is creating one family for Himself, comprising Jews and Gentiles. The animosity of Jews towards Gentiles was to cease; they were to be all one in Christ Jesus. Each member must walk in the steps of their father Abraham whose faith was such an example. This, Hebrews calls the 'better promises.'

So, the teaching of the principle of forgiveness through faith appears very early in the Bible. The better promises are first mentioned in Genesis chapter 12 when God first appeared to Abraham in Ur. Peter taught its significance when he said: *'You are sons of the prophets, and of the covenant which God made with our fathers, saying to Abraham, "And in your seed shall all the families of the earth be blessed."'* (Act 3:25)

So, in due time, the blessing upon all nations was bestowed by Jesus, first to the Jews and then to the nations: *'To you first, God, having raised up His Servant Jesus, sent Him to bless you, in turning away every one of you from your iniquities.'* (Acts 3:26) This promise was made long before the

Law and provided the blessing of forgiveness of sins. This, the Law could not do, because it was faulty.

Better promises made to Abraham

Abraham lived about 4,000 years ago in the city of Ur, in what today is Iraq but was then Chaldea. He was an idolater along with his fellow citizens (Josh. 24:2) but the God of glory appeared to him there (Acts 7:2) and made promises to him of huge significance. God said: *'I will make you into a great nation and I will bless you. I will make your name great, and you will be a blessing... and all peoples on earth will be blessed through you'.* (Gen. 12:2–3). The remarkable fact is that this man was elderly; he was childless and his wife was barren. Nonetheless he believed what God had told him and also obeyed the instruction to leave his home city and go to some unknown place to which God would lead him. Obviously, great trust was needed to abandon a settled way of life in a city to go forth into the unknown.

Abraham was led via Haran to Shechem, the centre of the land of Canaan, at which point God said: *'To your offspring I will give this land.'* (Gen. 12:7) It was a land full of Canaanites, yet Abraham believed what God said. Again, great faith was necessary to believe such a promise. Actually, we too are required to believe an even greater promise, that we are to inherit the earth, the Kingdom of God. When we think of the powerful nations like the United States of America and China which will have to be dispossessed to make way for us, we can grasp the magnitude of the promise.

Years passed and some of Abraham's experiences are recorded. They show his humanity, with which we can sympathise, but his chief worry was that, notwithstanding God's emphatic promises about becoming a great nation, still he had no child. When Abraham queried this with God, the reply came back: *'Look up at the sky and count the stars- if indeed you can count them. So shall your offspring be.'* Then the record continues: *'Abraham believed* the LORD, and he credited it to him for righteousness.' (Gen. 15:6 NIV)

Credited with righteousness

Paul used this important text when expounding the subject of justification by faith and said that God credited Abraham with righteousness not because he had done anything to deserve it, but simply because he believed what God had said and obeyed God's command. His obedience confirmed that he really did believe.

To emphasise what being credited with righteousness meant, Paul went on to quote from the Psalms (32:1–2) to show that the gift of righteousness equates to the forgiveness of sins. *'David says the same thing when he speaks of the blessedness of the one to whom God credits righteousness apart from works: Blessed are they whose transgressions are forgiven; whose sins are covered. Blessed is the one man whose sin the Lord will never count against them.'* (Rom. 4:6–8 NIV)

Paul next asks the question: *'Is this blessedness available to Abraham only?'* To which he answers in the negative and goes on to say: *'The words "it was credited to him" were written not for him alone, but also for us, to whom God will credit righteousness – for us who believe in him who raised Jesus our Lord from the dead.'* (Rom. 4:23–24 NIV)

The one who raised Jesus from the dead was God; therefore, if we believe Him, we too are given righteousness just like Abraham. Paul's reasoning is recorded in his letter to the Galatians as he encourages his readers to consider Abraham, who *'… believed God, and it was credited to him as righteousness. Understand, then that those who believe are children of Abraham. The Scripture foresaw that God would justify the Gentiles by faith, and announced the gospel in advance to Abraham: "All nations will be blessed through you." So those who have faith are blessed along with Abraham the man faith.'* (Gal. 3:6–9 NIV)

Then he continues with this startling thought: *'For you are all sons of God through faith in Christ Jesus. For as many of you as were baptized into Christ have put on Christ. There is neither Jew nor Greek, there is neither slave nor free, there is neither male nor female; for you are all one in Christ Jesus.'* (Galatians 3:26–29) So, having our sins forgiven by God, i.e., being justified by faith or having righteousness given to us, has far-reaching and wonderful consequences. We become God's children and heirs of the promises made to Abraham, no longer doomed to perish but able to look forward to eternal life. Paul has shown that this good news, or Gospel, was foreseen about 4,000 years ago, when God promised it to Abraham.

Salvation was never intended to be for the Jews only. The Jews, along with other peoples such as the descendants of Hagar and Keturah, claim natural descent from Abraham. However, the promises were to be through Isaac and at Mount Sinai, Isaac's seed through Jacob had been separated from all other peoples to receive God's revelation to mankind. With these privileges came the primary responsibility to believe and obey the words which God had entrusted to them.

The new and better covenant

Having looked at the 'better promises', we turn to the 'better covenant.' Had the old or first covenant been perfect or faultless, there would have been no need for a New Covenant.

The New Covenant is found in Jeremiah 31:31 and is quoted in full in this letter. It showed that the Old Covenant, the Law, was unable to save because of the faults in the people. They simply could not keep it (2 Chron. 34:21 and 35:18). The Law given at Sinai, formed the covenant which condemned them all. The New Covenant was very different. It did not require obedience to many detailed regulations, examples of which are found in Leviticus. However, the New Covenant called for God's people to 'know Him.' The remarkable fact is however, that the process begins with God calling the individual to 'know him'. Abraham was such a man to whom the God of glory appeared (Acts 7:2) and called him, a person who worshipped other gods (Josh. 24:2). Isaiah goes so far as to call Abraham God's friend (Isa. 41:8).   And concerning Moses, Exodus 33:11 says: *'The LORD spoke to Moses face to face, as a man speaks to his friend.'* When Moses asked the LORD to show him His glory, God did so and made Himself known to Moses saying: *'The Lord, the Lord God, merciful and gracious, longsuffering, and abounding in goodness and truth, keeping mercy for thousands, forgiving iniquity and transgression and sin, by no means clearing the guilty, visiting the iniquity of the fathers upon the children and the children's children to the third and the fourth generation.'* (Exo 34:6–7)

The character of the LORD contrasts profoundly with the gods of the heathen. After all, their gods were the product of their own imagination. These gods were to be feared and their wrath appeased. Pagan worshippers subjected themselves to cruel practices to make themselves worthy of their god's blessings. The offering of their children in the fire to Molech was a hideous example.   Israel often followed the practices of the pagans and were blind to the loving kindness of the LORD God who had delivered them from slavery.

'All shall know me'
The Greek word used for 'know' means to have understood or perceived. e.g. (John 14:6–7): *'Jesus said to Thomas, "I am the way, the truth, and the life. No one comes to the Father except through Me. If you had known Me, you would have known My Father also; and from now on you do know Him and have seen Him."'* Thomas had been one of Jesus' companions for three years and of course knew him, but, had not fully perceived who Jesus was and what his mission was really about as a manifestation of the character of His Father. Thomas was learning; he was acquiring knowledge and for that a different Greek word, *oida,* was used. But, under the New Covenant, all will know the LORD and appreciate His character. They will not need to be taught who the LORD is, and consequently, will walk in His paths.

The New Covenant was announced by Jeremiah in chapter 31:31-34 and quoted in full in Hebrews chapter 8:

> *"'Behold, the days are coming", says the LORD, "when I will make a new covenant with the house of Israel and with the house of Judah– not according to the covenant that I made with their fathers in the day when I took them by the hand to lead them out of the land of Egypt; because they did not continue in My covenant, and I disregarded them, says the LORD. For this is the covenant that I will make with the house of Israel after those days", says the LORD: "I will put My laws in their mind and write them on their hearts; and I will be their God, and they shall be My people. None of them shall teach his neighbour, and none his brother, saying, 'Know the LORD,' for all shall know Me, from the least of them to the greatest of them. For I will be merciful to their unrighteousness, and their sins and their lawless deeds I will remember no more."'* (Heb. 8:8–12)

This covenant is guaranteed by Almighty Creator, the one who gave the sun by day and the moon and stars by night to give light. He is the LORD of Hosts, the one who also stirs up the waves of sea so that they roar. It is inconceivable that these awesome wonders should ever cease, and the certainty of the New Covenant is comparable. The guarantee is reinforced by the LORD with this challenge *'If heaven above can be measured, and the foundations of the earth searched out beneath, I will also cast off all the seed of Israel...'* (Jer. 31: 37) Man's exploration of the universe in our day shows these assurances to be infinitely greater than the heavens as seen by the naked eye in Jeremiah's day.

Returning to Hebrews 8:13, the following deduction is made. Because the prophet said *'A New Covenant',* it naturally follows that the first covenant with Israel was obsolete and on the point of utter destruction. The language in this verse is very strong and means complete desolation, ruin. Jeremiah witnessed the

Temple's total destruction by the Babylonians. He saw it torn down and burned with fire. Now the day was fast approaching when the huge temple standing in Paul's day would be brought to ruin by the Romans. It was not generally Roman policy to destroy valuable assets such as towns and cities. It was because of the fanatical determination of the Jews to defend the city that the Romans were forced to bring it to utter ruin.

Digression: When and why did the Law vanish away?

We have seen that God's promises to Abraham from the start said that all families of the earth would be blessed in him on the basis of faith. God separated Abraham's descendants through Isaac and Jacob to be His special people. Through them, He would show the nations how blessed a godly nation would be, so that all nations would want to seek Israel's God (Deut. 4:5–8). Israel was given the Law which was intended to educate them and govern their lives before God. Galatians 3:23–26 explains that Israel was kept under supervision by the Law until Christ had come; then the principle of forgiveness of sins through faith in him was revealed.

So, God's plan of salvation had reached the stage at which He would call many sons, not just from Israel but from all families of the earth. Christ Jesus had come and had overcome the power of sin through his perfect life, death and resurrection. Justification was now offered to all who put their faith in Christ Jesus. The Law had served its purpose in bringing Israel from childhood to maturity and was now redundant.

The Law as a tutor had a profound weakness as is explained in Galatians 3:10–14. The Law cursed everyone who did not keep all of it. Since no one could keep it, no one could claim to be without sin. Furthermore, Habakkuk states that the just will live by faith whereas the Law stipulated that the man who kept the Law would live, but that had proved impossible. So, the wonderful news was that Christ has saved us from the curse of the Law. Christ was cursed for us in that the Law cursed anyone hanged on a tree.

Upon his resurrection, the blessing of Abraham became available to all nations through faith in Christ.

The letter to the Galatians was written for the same reason as the letter to the Hebrews. It very firmly rebuked those Jews in the ecclesia who were seeking to undermine the Gospel of Salvation in Christ Jesus in order to re-establish the Law. Such a move would be futile. What was the use of going back to a system which cursed rather than saved? The Law was glorious, but it was passing away to be replaced by something much more glorious (2 Cor. 3:10–11). A far better way had been provided giving hope to Gentiles as well as Jews. No doubt this change offended the Jews who saw themselves as God's elite people and despised the Gentiles. But Scripture showed that Jews and Gentiles alike were all condemned as sinners: *'But the Scripture has confined all under sin, that the promise by faith in Jesus Christ might be given to those who believe.'* (Gal 3:22)

A very serious point is made in Galatians 5:4: *'You have become estranged from Christ, you who attempt to be justified by law; you have fallen from grace.'* Paul likened the Law to a husband. The wife is bound to her husband whilst he is alive, but if he dies, she is free to marry another. So he says: *'But now we have been delivered from the law, having died to what we were held by, so that we should serve in the newness of the Spirit and not in the oldness of the letter.'* (Rom. 7:6) He also wrote to the Colossians that Jesus: *'having wiped out the handwriting of requirements that was against us, which was contrary to us. And He has taken it out of the way, having nailed it to the cross.'* (Col. 2:14) His death also wiped-out sins committed under the Law (Heb. 9:15).

The Law had been made obsolete. Nonetheless many Christian Jews still lived according to the Law and their own traditions and tried to insist on the Gentile believers doing the same. However, in AD70 the temple and the city of Jerusalem were destroyed. There was, therefore, no place to offer gifts and sacrifices and nowhere for the priests to minister. But between the resurrection of Christ and AD70 the Law continued to be kept by Jewish Christians. Some of them were priests whose role had been made redundant and they were now creating tensions in the ecclesias. An example is recorded in Acts 21:20 in which the elders of the Jerusalem ecclesia took Paul to task and said very many Jews have believed and are all zealous for the Law. But they have been told that Jews living among the Gentiles should forsake Moses and no longer circumcise their children.

This complaint was true, as Paul's letter to the Galatians shows. (Gal 3:10–15; 5:1–4) A meeting was called to discuss the issue which reached the agreement that the Gentiles were not expected to keep the Law. However, Paul's case is put clearly in his letter to the Philippians: *'Beware,'* he writes, *'of dogs,'* that is Jews who were insisting on the need for Gentile believers to be circumcised. Circumcision should be of the heart, not the flesh, said Paul. He explains that this means that we worship God in spirit and rejoice in Christ Jesus rather than boasting in circumcision of the flesh. He had every reason to have confidence in the flesh, but since knowing Jesus, he rated all that as rubbish. Paul knew he had gained far more, that through faith in Christ he had been given righteousness by God. This was not a righteousness of his own gained by obedience to the Law, but it came through knowing Christ and the power of his resurrection (paraphrase of Phil.3:1–11).

Paul explained in Romans chapter 7 that even though *'the law is holy, and the commandment holy and just and good',* the fact remained that the law exposed man's innate sinfulness.

9 THE RITES AND SACRIFICES OF THE LAW

AN EXPOSITION OF HEBREWS CHAPTER 9

In Hebrews chapter 8 we examined the New Covenant. This covenant promised that sins could be forgiven, and it therefore differed profoundly from the Old Covenant – the Law of Moses. The Old Covenant, ratified by the blood of sacrificed animals, pointed out sins and reminded people of their sinfulness (Ex. 24:5–7).

The New Covenant was foreseen in God's covenant with Abraham. It showed that sinners could be counted righteous through faith in God. This was long before the giving of the Law through Moses.

Now chapter 9 teaches that the tabernacle built under the first covenant was a teaching tool. Later in this chapter it is spoken of as a copy of the real tabernacle in the heavens. It was to illustrate something far greater and was only a figure of the real house of God in the heavens.

It can be seen, therefore, that the Most Holy Place was a figure of heaven itself. The High Priest went into the Most Holy, into the figurative presence of God, once a year to seek forgiveness for the unintentional sins of himself and all the people. The rules for him were very strict and contravention meant death.

The real priest is Jesus; he is the substance and not a shadow, immortal and in possession of divine nature. He has already entered into the presence of God and is seated at His right hand, where he intercedes on behalf of his brothers and sisters.

We have already been taught in many ways how much better Jesus is as our great High Priest. He had nothing to do with the High Priests under the Law of Moses. He was from a non-priestly tribe. He was a priest in the order of Melchizedec, an order that existed long before the Law. He lives for ever. He did not succeed following the death of a previous priest, but was specifically appointed by God with an oath.

The altar of incense

We are familiar with the furniture of the tabernacle and Paul describes the pieces in this chapter. However, verses 3–4 are puzzling. Paul says that the altar of incense was within the Most Holy. He also says that the ark of the covenant was there and describes the contents of the ark. We know that the altar of incense or golden censer as the A.V. translates it, was not in the Holy of Holies. It stood before the curtain that separated the Holy from the Most Holy. So why does Paul make what seems to be an elementary mistake? Divine inspiration does not make mistakes, so we need to discover why Paul made this statement.

Bro. John Carter in his book *Letter to the Hebrews* makes the following comment:

> 'In principle, the altar of incense belonged to the Most Holy Place.' The design details were not given in the section which describes all the other furniture in the Holy Place. i.e. Exodus 25. Instead, the details are to be found in Exodus 30. Its proximity to the ark of the covenant is described like this*: 'And you shall put it in front of the veil that is above the ark of the testimony, in front of the mercy seat that is above the testimony, where I will meet with you.'* (Ex. 30:6) So, in principle the altar of incense is linked with the mercy seat upon which God figuratively sat enthroned.'

In the description of Solomon's temple, the altar of incense is said to belong to the Most Holy Place: '*also he overlaid with gold the entire altar that was by the inner sanctuary.*' (1 Kings 6:22) Again, we find the same association of the altar of incense and the ark in Exodus 30:10 and Leviticus 16:15–19. The blood of atonement was sprinkled on both. Revelation 8:3 makes the same close association when speaking of the altar of incense being before the throne.

Another detail which must be significant is the observation in 1 Kings 8:9 that there was nothing in the ark except the two stone tablets on which was written the words of the covenant. The golden pot containing the sample of manna and Aaron's rod that budded were no longer there. The manna was a memorial of the LORD's unique provision of bread for His people until the entrance into the Promised Land (Ex. 16:34). Aaron's rod, however, may not have been placed in the ark but 'before it'. The size of the ark tends to that view.

The better High Priest

We notice that Hebrews 9 alludes to the Day of Atonement and the function of the High Priest. The letter draws particular attention to the superiority of Jesus as High Priest of the New Covenant. So, comparing the Old and the New Covenants, Paul says that the priests went into the Holy Place to minister before God, but never did they enter the Most Holy. The High Priest entered alone on one day of the year only, the Day of Atonement. On that day he went in twice, first with the blood of the bullock for himself and secondly, with the blood of the goat for the sins of the people committed in ignorance. In this way, the Holy Spirit showed that the way into the Most Holy was not yet open to all. The veil was drawn to hide the way of redemption in Christ that would be revealed in God's predetermined time (Heb. 9:6–8). Whilst the Old Covenant arrangements were still in place, the blessing of the New Covenant, the forgiveness of sins, was still to come.

So, the point is made that while the tabernacle was in use for the offering of sacrifices for sins and gifts to God, the offerer's conscience could never be made perfect. These sacrifices were rituals, though full of meaning, involving foods and drinks, various washings, and onerous laws imposed on the Levitical priests until the time of reformation. Reformation is better translated as rectification, that is putting things right that are wrong. It alludes to the breakdown of relations caused by Adam's transgression. That which heals that breach is the 'New Covenant' and that new order had arrived. It brought the possibility of peace with God instead of animosity. How nonsensical therefore, to cling to the old order of the Mosaic Law, when a very much better way was offered by God which would give life instead of death.

Christ entered the real house of God with his own blood, once only. This retrospectively purified the consciences of those of faith who lived under the Law, thus enabling them to partake of the eternal promises of God. Such characters are mentioned in Psalm 42:1–2 as those who thirst for the living God as a deer pants for flowing streams.

Now it was possible to meet God and receive the promise of eternal inheritance; an inheritance that Peter says can never perish, spoil or fade (1 Pet. 1:4 NIV). If animals' blood could render clean some defilement of the body, how much more so the blood of Christ, which purifies the whole person by the washing away of sin, by casting sins away as far as the east is from the west.

Forgiveness was now available to those under the Old Covenant, providing they had sought to follow God's precepts because they loved Him and trusted His promises. Faithful to God in obeying the law, not merely as rituals with tiresome restrictions to be endured, but in a real belief in God's presence among them. Faith was the essence, faith such as Abraham had. Sadly, this was not understood by most of them. As Hebrews 4:2 had already said, the good tidings about Jesus was taught in the Law, but it was not effective in them because it was not mixed with faith

Wills and covenants

The next verse (Heb. 9:16) as translated in the AV is confusing, as it appears not to follow logically from what goes before and does not help the exposition. It has been the subject of much discussion. The context is paramount. As we have seen again and again, the letter is contrasting the Old Covenant with the New Covenant. *'For where there is a testament, there must also of necessity be the death of the testator.'* (Heb. 9:16) This translation from the NKJV follows the A.V., as do other English translations in introducing the idea of wills, testaments and testators.

Two points must be noted concerning the words translated 'will' and 'testator'. The Greek word translated 'will' is *diatheke*. However, the letter to the Hebrews is addressed to Jews and the corresponding Hebrew word is *berith* which means 'covenant'. *Diatheke* is the word used by Jesus in instituting the memorial feast. *'This cup is the new covenant in My blood...'* (Luke 22:20) and *'this is my blood of the new covenant'* (Mark 14:24). Paul uses the same word in 1 Corinthians 11:25 *'This cup is the new covenant in my blood.'* W.E. Vine in his Expository Dictionary of New Testament Words has this to say:

> 'In covenant making, the sacrifice of a victim was customary. He who made a covenant did so at the cost of a life. While the terminology in Heb.9:16,17 has the appearance of being appropriate to the making of a will, there is excellent reason for adhering to the meaning 'covenant making.' The rendering "the death of the testator" would make Christ a Testator, which He was not. He did not die simply that the terms of a testamentary disposition might be fulfilled for the heirs. Here he who is the "the mediator of a New Covenant" is Himself the victim whose death was necessary.'

In Genesis 15 the making of a covenant is described in the covenant God made with Abraham. Abraham was instructed to bring a heifer three years old, a female goat three years old, a ram three years old, a turtledove, and a young pigeon. All were cut in half except the birds. Then he drove away the birds of prey which fell upon the carcases and as the sun set, he fell into deep sleep. In the darkness of night, a smoking firepot and a flaming torch passed between the carcases. The record states that on that day the LORD made a covenant with Abraham. It is evident that this covenant was made by the shedding of blood. Three three-year old animals were cut in two, along with two birds which were not divided. The covenant makers walked between the pieces, God in the figures of the smoking fire pot and the flaming torch.

Another example is of King Zedekiah who made a covenant in which the people joined him in a commitment to release their fellow Israelites from slavery. No sooner had this covenant been made than it was broken, and the freed men were seized and again enslaved. Jeremiah was moved to say that those men who had broken their commitment would themselves become like the calf that they had cut in two when making the covenant (Jer. 34:18).

Young's concordance always translates *diatheke* as 'covenant' and in his Literal Translation of the Bible he recognizes the Hebrew context of the subject, i.e. that *diatheke* is a translation of the Hebrew word *berith* meaning covenant.

The Greek word *diatithemi* is translated 'testator' meaning 'one who makes a covenant'. So Young uses the phrase 'covenant victim' (the sacrifice by which the covenant was confirmed) and translates verses 16– 17 thus: *'for where a covenant is, the death of the covenant-victim to come in is necessary, for a covenant over dead victims is steadfast, since it is no force at all when the covenant victim liveth.'*

So, there seems to be no logical reason for translating 'diatheke' as 'will' in verse 17 which is a single exception to the rest of the New Testament, where it is translated 'covenant'.

It is worth noting that in the Septuagint *diatheke* is the word invariably used when translating 'covenant' from the Hebrew..

Jesus' blood confirmed the New Covenant

Seen in a Jewish context, the next verses follow on logically. Jesus was the covenant sacrifice or victim. It was his blood which ratified or sealed the New Covenant. The first covenant was ratified by the blood of animals, water, scarlet wool and hyssop. Moses sprinkled the blood on the altar, the book of the covenant and the people and proclaimed *'This is the blood of the covenant which God has commanded you.'* He proceeded to sprinkle the tabernacle and its vessels. Paul explained that according to the Law, almost everything could be purified by blood and that without the shedding of blood, there could be no forgiveness of sin.

Therefore it was necessary that the copies of the things in the heavens should be purified with these, but the heavenly things themselves with better sacrifices than these'. (Heb 9:23)

The Old Covenant with its book of the law, the people, tent, furnishings, priesthood etc was purified by the sprinkling of the blood of calves and goats, but these were only copies or types of the real heavenly things. Jesus' blood, shed as the victim for the making of the New Covenant, enabled the promises made by his Father for the salvation of the faithful. The promises, concerning the seed through whom all nations would be blessed, and the son who would build a house for God and rule his Father's kingdom for ever, could now proceed to fulfilment.

Entry into the covenant for all nations is explained in Ephesians 2:12–13 where speaking of the Gentiles: *'at that time you were without Christ, being aliens from the commonwealth of Israel and strangers from the covenants* (N.B. *diatheke*) *of promise, having no hope and without God in the world. But now in Christ Jesus you who once were far off have been brought near by the blood of Christ.'* (See also Gal 3:26-29)

Jesus' better sacrifice

As we have already noted, Jesus' sacrifice was made once when he was crucified, whereas the Levitical High Priest had to make a sacrifice every year in order to be allowed entry into the Most Holy Place. Paul then argues that this fact demonstrates the superior nature of Christ's sacrifice, since otherwise *'He then would have had to suffer often since the foundation of the world; but now, once at the end of the ages, He has appeared to put away sin by the sacrifice of Himself.'* (Heb. 9:26) *'At the end of the ages'* I take to mean the end of the age which began when sin entered the world and Jesus was foreseen as the *'seed of the woman'*, ending when he rose from the dead.

Jesus is coming to judge

'And as it is appointed for men to die once, but after this the judgment, so Christ was offered once to bear the sins of many. To those who eagerly wait for Him He will appear a second time, apart from sin, for salvation.' (Heb. 9:27–28)

This is a very serious exhortation to prompt careful self-examination. Jesus is coming again to judge between the righteous and the unrighteous, the faithful and the unfaithful. If some of the Hebrews had abandoned him for the law and counted his sacrifice as worthless, then they had every reason to be very fearful. They would have been familiar with the words of Daniel when he spoke of an unparalleled time of distress, when those of his people would be spared, all those whose names are found written in the Book. Of those sleeping in the dust of the earth many will awake, some to everlasting life, but some to shame and everlasting disgrace. There was still time for the Hebrews to think again, turn wholeheartedly to Jesus Christ and join those longing for his return and the joyful day of salvation.

10 THE LAW ONLY A SHADOW

AN EXPOSITION OF HEBREWS CHAPTER 10

'For the law, having a shadow of the good things to come, and not the very image of the things, can never with these same sacrifices, which they offer continually year by year make those who approach, perfect.' (Heb. 10:1)

A shadow is a dark area or shape produced by a body coming between rays of light and a surface. Depending on the angle of the light falling on the body obstructing it, the shadow will be a more or less distorted silhouette. The first sentence of chapter 10 says that the law was only a shadow. It taught important principles but was only a preliminary step. In due time God would reveal not a mere shadow but the real body casting the shadow. During the shadow period the real body or the substance, was a mystery or secret. The point of this letter is that the reality had now been revealed. We are no longer looking at a shadow but at the actual body, and that body is Christ, the light of the world.

The purpose of the law

The purpose of God in giving the Law is explained by Paul in Galatians 3:19–25. It was given to define transgressions, but only until the coming of the promised Seed through whom all nations would be blessed. The promised blessing was the forgiveness of transgressions through faith. Had the law been able to provide forgiveness and life, then God's promises to Abraham and his seed would have been irrelevant. But the law exposed the sinfulness of mankind and thereby the justice of God in condemning man to death. The Law demonstrated that all who were under it were sinners. The promise of life through faith in Jesus Christ to those who believe appears in brilliant contrast to the Law.

Before faith came, Israel were allowed no freedom by the Law, but were being looked after until justification by faith was revealed. The Law performed the role of a guardian, teaching Israel in a shadowy way about the coming of Christ. The marvellous purpose of God to justify them by faith in Abraham's seed had now come, and so the guardian's role was no longer needed. This point is made clear in Colossians 2:13–14. They had, in effect, been dead, condemned to die because of their transgressions. Although they had been circumcised according to the Law, that Law showed how sinful they were, in fact, demonstrating that in reality, they were morally uncircumcised. But through baptism into Christ, that old man of sin died and rose again as a new man. Jesus had made him alive together with him, having forgiven him all his trespasses. At the same time he had wiped out those laws which so often tripped the old man up, taking them out of the way and nailing them to the cross. Therefore the preliminary stage of God's plan for Israel, the guardianship stage, came to an end with the death of Jesus.

This wonderful transformation was very dramatically shown by the tearing of the veil of the temple from top to bottom, exposing the ark and the cherubim at the very moment in which Jesus gave up the spirit. This would have been a horrifying sight for those who had engineered the death of Jesus. News of it would have travelled throughout Jerusalem like wildfire and would be feared as an appalling portent. It coincided with an earthquake and an unnatural darkness. The news of these terrifying events would have been taken back by the crowds of visitors from across the world. It may well explain why the authorities accepted the fact of Jesus' resurrection so quickly, bribing the guards to spread abroad a futile story about the disciples stealing the body. The authorities had been thoroughly shaken up!

Now, the once self-important priesthood found the Most Holy exposed to view and the role of the High Priest, as the only man permitted to pass through the veil on the Day of Atonement was suddenly gone. Perhaps this is what Paul meant when he wrote that Jesus had disarmed principalities and powers, (the Jewish hierarchy?) making a public spectacle of them, triumphing over them in it (Col. 2:15–17). The Jewish rulers, the teachers of the law, those scribes and Pharisees who despised and oppressed the poor and uneducated, were suddenly shown up for what they were. Thus, were they put to shame. It also explains their hatred of the followers of Jesus. The apostles persistently accused them of killing the Son of God. They could not deny it, confronted by the empty tomb, and the miracles, wonders and signs done by God through the apostles and other Christians. So, their only recourse was to attempt to destroy them by ruthless persecution. The example of Saul of Tarsus illustrates the violence used. Even though Saul was reformed by the Lord's appearance to him on the Damascus Road, their attempts to undermine Jewish Christians by bringing them back to the Law is what this letter to the Hebrews so powerfully sets out to counteract.

Deficiencies of the Law

Paul continues to point out the deficiencies of the Law with quotations from Psalm 40. This Psalm foresaw that Jesus knew God did not want burnt offerings and sacrifices for sins; they were not pleasing to Him. The Psalm continues by expressing Jesus' words that he would proclaim the good news of righteousness in the great assembly. The good news of righteousness was nothing less than the Gospel of Salvation proclaimed by Jesus throughout the land. The people were dumfounded by this new teaching and by the wonderful miracles, signs and wonders which God did through him.

Psalm 40 revealed a stark contrast between Jesus and Israel; Jesus came to do the will of God, whereas the Psalm says of those who scoffed at Jesus: *'Let them be confounded because of their shame…'* (v. 15) God was wearied by Israel's empty religious gestures; they had become a burden to Him. But here was a man with whom He was well pleased, who said: *'Behold, I have come to do your will.'* This is the body God had prepared which would be the perfect, unblemished sacrifice offered in sincerity and truth.

So much better...

That sacrifice, as forseen in type in Abraham and Isaac, was made by God and by Jesus. It was the man who was sacrificed, not an animal who had no consciousness of sin or death. Adam was taught the vivid lesson, which was continued under the law, that the sinner's death could only be deferred by the pouring out of the life blood of an animal instead of his own. No wonder animal sacrifices could never take away sins: *'For it is not possible that the blood of bulls and goats could take away sins.'* (Heb. 10:4)

So Paul continues in verse 9 by saying that God had set the first arrangement aside to be replaced by the new, in which sanctification was achieved through the single sacrifice of Jesus. It was a sacrifice which did not need to be repeated, for it was completely effective. This is the point made at the beginning of the chapter. The Law with its many repetitive sacrifices could not achieve what the one sacrifice of Christ did. Under the Law, the worshipper could never forget his sinfulness and the need to offer sacrifice. But Christ's sacrifice is altogether different. It does not set out to continually remind us that we are sinners. Rather, it reminds us that we are under grace, that God gives righteousness to those who love Him. This sacrifice was not an animal offered instead of the sinner, but a perfect man, God's beloved son. So, *'... by one offering He has perfected forever those who are being sanctified.'* (Heb. 10:14)

What a marvellous fact to grasp and understand! Surely it means that a believer should not be weighed down with a sense of guilt, worrying himself with questions like: 'Am I good enough to be in the Kingdom?'; 'Have I done enough in service to God?' God and Jesus have done everything necessary to make us perfect. Faith in this marvellous principle is God's way of saving a believer. Abraham believed God and it was counted to him as righteousness and that vital fact was written down for his sake and also for our sakes. We too, will be counted righteous if we believe in Him who raised up Jesus our Lord from the dead, who was sacrificed for our sins, and raised for our justification. Faith however, must be mixed with works as evidence of the sincerity of the believer.

Faith must be mixed with works

Like Abraham, our response must be to give glory to God for what the sacrifice of His son has done for us. It is this wholehearted appreciation which should motivate obedient behaviour. It must be understood that it is Christ who has made the effective sacrifice, a sacrifice which is able to make us perfect. We must not fall into the Jewish way of thinking, and the common human way of thinking, that we must make sacrifices for our sins. That is the basis of paganism – we have to earn salvation to appease an angry God. The truth is that it is God who has made the sacrifice, to save us. (John 3:16–17) *'For God so loved the world that He gave His only begotten Son, that whoever believes in Him should not perish but have everlasting life. For God did not send His Son into the world to condemn the world, but that the world through Him might be saved.'*

Notice a detail in Hebrews 10:12 that the man whose one sacrifice is so effective is seated at the right hand of God. Again Paul compares the High Priest under the Law with Jesus.

The High Priest under the Law always stood to carry out his duties. It was a ceaseless duty, one year after another the same procedure was required of him. But Christ, in offering himself as the perfect sacrifice, sat down. He had done all that God required once and for all, *'from that time waiting till his enemies are made his footstool.'* (quoting from Psalm 110).

In verse 16 Paul again refers to Jeremiah 31 to make an important point. When Israel received the covenant at Mount Sinai they said: *'All that the Lord has spoken we will do and be obedient.'* Of course, they could not do what they had promised. Under the New Covenant it is not what the people say that counts but what God says: *'their sins and their lawless deeds I will remember no more.'*

Hence *'where there is remission of these, there is no longer an offering for sin.'*

So, we must be reminded, that it is faith in God that pleases Him, not sacrifices offered under the Law. What would be the point in offering sacrifices for sin if they had already been forgiven? So, another thought follows:

> *Therefore, brethren, having boldness to enter the Holiest by the blood of Jesus, by a new and living way which He consecrated for us, through the veil, that is, His flesh, and having a High Priest over the house of God, let us draw near with a true heart in full assurance of faith, having our hearts sprinkled from an evil conscience and our bodies washed with pure water.'* (Heb. 10:19-22)

There are some very reassuring principles expressed here: -

We should enter the presence of our heavenly Father boldly, that is without fear, because we do so through Jesus. Jesus gave his life for our salvation and intercedes with His Father for our forgiveness. Since our Father gave His son for the same reason, why should we be fearful in the presence of so much love?

Jesus has been specially consecrated to provide that access to the Father. The Tabernacle as a type is used to illustrate this point. The veil separated the Most Holy from the Holy; no one could go through the veil except the High Priest, and that only once per year, but the veil stood for Jesus' flesh. It is through Jesus that we are permitted access to the antitypical Most Holy. That fact, as we have already mentioned, was emphatically indicated by the veil of the temple being ripped apart from top to bottom at the death of Jesus.

To all this we can add that through baptism into Christ we become one with his body, (Gal 3:27–28) a body with Christ as its head and we as its members. (1 Cor 12:12–27). The metaphor appears again in Ephesians 2:4–6: *'But God, who is rich in mercy, because of His great love with which He loved us, even when we were dead in trespasses, made us alive together with Christ (by grace you have been saved), and raised us up together, and made us sit together in the heavenly places in Christ Jesus.'*

Notice that God has *'made us sit together in heavenly places in Christ Jesus.'* The implications are amazing. We saw in Hebrews 1 that Jesus sat down at the right hand of the Father, whereas the angels stood. Furthermore, because we are metaphorically part of Christ's body, we are said to be seated in the presence of God in the real Most Holy. If the reality of this figure was always in our minds, we would do our utmost to be very well behaved.

Practical application

Following this inspiring teaching comes the practical application of its principles. Obviously, this does not give us the right to sin with impunity. *'Let us draw near with a true heart in full assurance of faith, having our hearts sprinkled from an evil conscience and our bodies washed with pure water.'* (Heb. 10:22) This is a reference to baptism and also an allusion to the washing of the priests under the Law, but it is not just the body which is washed; it is the heart also. This reminds us again of the New Covenant, in which God puts His laws in our hearts and writes them on our minds. To draw near with a true heart implies repentance and belief in God's willingness to forgive. A true heart does not presume that it can continue in sin and be forgiven (Rom. 6:1).

So, we should not be weighed down by a consciousness of our sins because they are forgiven by God. The one who intercedes on our behalf is none other than the one who laid down his life for our salvation. Our sins once forgiven cease to exist. Scripture uses such expressions as *'blotted out'*; *'washed away'*; *'cast as far as the east is from the west'*; *'remembered no more'*.

If we are moved by an awareness of the marvellous things God has done for us, then we shall want to respond with love. Such love is seen in practice by the behaviour described in verses 23–24: *'Let us hold fast the confession of our hope without wavering, for He who promised is faithful. And let us consider one another in order to stir up love and good works'* To 'stir up' or 'provoke' comes from the Greek *paroxymos.* It is the word from which the English word 'paroxysm' derives. The Oxford dictionary defines this as 'a sudden attack or outburst of a particular emotion or activity'. It is the love of God which causes such a paroxysm, or as Jesus said: *'You shall love the Lord your God with all your heart and with all your soul and with all your mind. This is the first and great commandment. And a second is like it: You shall love your neighbour as yourself.'* (Matt. 22:37–39)

How does this work in practice? It springs from the paroxysm, caused by the wonder we feel for all God has done for us. We are moved to joy at the hope set before us; it comes from the stimulus of the word of God; the thrill we get from sharing the word. It is why we meet together frequently, stimulating one another to the love of God. Hence the next lesson: *'not forsaking the assembling of ourselves together, as is the manner of some, but exhorting one another, and so much the more as you see the Day approaching.'* (10:25)

'Assembling of ourselves together'

In the Greek, *Synagogue* means a 'gathering of people', but the word used by Paul comes from a related Greek word *epi-sun-agogue* which means a 'complete gathering of people'. It is used in only one other place in the New Testament which is 2 Thessalonians 2:1: *'Now, brethren, concerning the coming of our Lord Jesus Christ and our gathering together to Him.'* Jesus will not be careless in gathering to himself his brothers and sisters. He will not overlook a few here and there; it will be a complete gathering. It will be the whole body of Christ which will be assembled on that day. If we are not eager to be a part of Christ's body now, we cannot expect to part of him on that day.

We also take note that the purpose of assembling together is to exhort one another. The Greek word translated 'exhorting' is the verb of the noun *parakletos,* the word used by Jesus in the Gospel of John where it is translated as 'comforter.' Its meaning is that of coming to one another to aid, to comfort and give succour. When Jesus used it, he was promising his apostles that when he left them, he would send them the spirit of truth to help them; to enable them to recall all that he had taught them, and to guide them into all truth. (John 16:7–14)

The importance of assembling for such a purpose is obvious *'and so much the more as you see the day approaching.'* Of course, Jesus' brothers and sisters were scattered abroad and assembled in small companies, but they were to understand that they were parts of the same body.

So, in the context of the letter to the Hebrews, the force of the exhortation is this: *'For if we sin wilfully after we have received the knowledge of the truth, there no longer remains a sacrifice for sins…'* (v. 26) In other words, if you abandon the body of Christ and return to the assembly of those who adhered to the Law of Moses, then of course, there is no sacrifice for sins. The Law was now redundant and obsolete and its sacrifices useless. Forgiveness was now through faith in the sacrifice of Christ, *'who was delivered up because of our offenses, and was raised because of our justification.'* (Rom. 4:25) To treat the sacrifice of Christ with such disrespect could lead only to *'a certain fearful expectation of judgment, and fiery indignation which will devour the adversaries. Anyone who has rejected Moses' law dies without mercy on the testimony of two or three witnesses. Of how much worse punishment, do you suppose, will he be thought worthy who has trampled the Son of God underfoot, counted the blood of the covenant by which he was sanctified a common thing, and insulted the Spirit of grace?' 'For we know Him who said, "Vengeance is mine, I will repay," says the Lord. And again, "The Lord will judge His people." It is a fearful thing to fall into the hands of the living God.'* (10:27–31)

This final quotation is like a hammer blow. They would remember that these were the words of God through Moses (Deut.32:35) and the context is awful. There Israel is referred to as a nation without sense and without discernment. If only they were wise and would understand and discern what their end will be. They abandoned the God who made them and rejected the Rock their Saviour.

The case could not be put more strongly. Paul exposes the absurdity of it in Galatians 4:9: *'But now after you have known God, or rather are known by God, how is it that you turn again to the weak and beggarly elements, to which you desire again to be in bondage?'* 'Weak' means 'impotent' and 'beggarly' means 'poverty stricken'. Would any rational person want to be in bondage to such a system having once tasted the liberty of being in Christ?

Having delivered such a powerful exhortation, Paul does his utmost to encourage their response. Remember how you had once been wholehearted members of the body of Christ, when, newly enlightened, you faced the challenge of much suffering and still held firm. Some of you were abused and tortured to make a public show, while others stood loyally with them. You shared the sufferings of the prisoners and cheerfully accepted the seizure of your possessions, because you knew that you possessed something better and more lasting. So, Paul comes to the crux of the matter when he exhorts them not to throw away their confidence in Jesus, for it will be far more rewarding. You need to endure these hardships if you are to do God's will and win what he has promised. Very soon, and here Paul quotes Habakkuk: *'... he who is coming will come and will not delay. But my righteous one will live by faith. And I take no pleasure in the one who shrinks back. But we do not belong to those who shrink back and are destroyed, but to those who have faith and are saved.'* (Heb. 10:37-39)

Would anyone choose such an option having once been enlightened? Sadly, the answer is yes. The Scriptures show this to be a fact again and again, and our own experience confirms the truth of it. The relevance of chapter 11, the faith chapter, is now obvious.

The climax of the letter

The letter has reached its climax. That impassioned appeal is followed by examples of people who had exhibited faith in God's promises. But, notice how from Abel onwards, many of those examples lived long before the Law was given as a guardian to Israel. Obviously, the Law, because it did not exist, could not have saved them. Their salvation was by faith through the grace of God. God taught Abraham that he was counted righteous because he believed Him, and furthermore was called the friend of God! (James 2:23)

11 THE GREAT CLOUD OF WITNESSES

AN EXPOSITION OF HEBREWS CHAPTER 11

The Hebrew Christian knew that faith meant belief in God's word. However, they did need reminding that the present order of things would pass away and that something far better was promised. All the examples given by Paul are of people who obviously did believe that because their actions showed it to be so. Faced with death, they did not complain that their hopes had been dashed. In fact they all died in faith without receiving the things promised, but looked forward in hope.

Faith is confidence in God's promises

Faith is an abstract quality rather than something tangible and is discerned by a person's behaviour. Faith is having confidence in the one who gave him his hope. Even though the hope is invisible at present, the man of faith is certain of its coming to pass. To believe the hope to be real and reliable requires faith, that is trust in God. The sight of the eyes has always been prime evidence as proof that something or someone exists, but to believe in someone and something which cannot be seen as yet, needs faith. The examples which follow are those who were commended because they had such faith and showed their trust in God by the way they lived.

The first example requiring faith is the momentous one of creation as recorded in Genesis chapter one. For us, living in the last days, it is such an important truth to believe and defend against the false prophets of science. By faith we believe that the universe was fashioned by the word of God. God spoke ten times (Gen. 1:3, 6, 9, 11, 14, 20 ,24 ,26, 28 and 29) and all that we see and know about His creation came to pass. The visible that we can see (the evidence of our eyes) was created by the word of God. So, faith is not required to believe that the world exists. It is plainly visible and fills us with wonder. It is in the invisible Creator's existence that faith is necessary. Indeed, verse 6 goes further, because without faith we cannot please our Creator. Furthermore, if we do not believe in His existence, it is futile to look for Him. Not only must we believe that God created all things by His word, creating out of nothing the wonderful things we see with our eyes, we must also believe that He will reward those who believe and search for Him. Yet, the people of the country in which we are strangers and pilgrims refuse the evidence of their eyes and fail to acknowledge the Creator's hand in the things they see. As Paul tried to persuade the citizens of Lystra: *'Nevertheless He* [God] *did not leave Himself without witness, in that He did good, gave us rain from heaven and fruitful seasons, filling our hearts with food and gladness...'* (Act 14:17)

Mankind's fast-growing knowledge of the extraordinary beauty and complexity of creation should compel admiration of the designer and His creative ability. Mankind ought to understand that his own creativity is but a reflection of the infinitely greater creativity of his Creator. Man's pride refuses to allow such an obvious conclusion. He has always preferred to worship the things he himself has imagined and made with his own hands. He would be insulted and regard as insane, anyone who refused to believe that something he had designed and made, however simple, was produced by pure chance.

God is not ashamed to be called our God

There are some amazing things in this chapter which are hard for a believer to digest. Hebrews 11:16 says that *'God is not ashamed to be called their God.'* God is not embarrassed to be associated with us if we believe Him and is not offended that we call Him our God. Indeed, we have already read that God is pleased with those who search for Him. It is difficult to think of greater encouragement. Nevertheless, Scripture reassures us again and again that we are His children, He is our Father and that He gave His beloved and perfect son to die for us, so that we might be reconciled to Him. God has done everything to enable us to draw close to Him so that He can give us the wonderful things He has promised. Ought we not to expect God to seek pleasure in the works of His hands by interacting with mankind?

Having such a loving God, we are not like those who do not know Him. For them, life is so fleeting that they must make the most of it and hold on to it tenaciously. In contrast, those with hope know that when losing a beloved believer, overriding the grief and bereavement is the assurance of resurrection to a vastly superior life. None of those commemorated for their faith in this chapter have yet entered upon the promised inheritance. With us in mind, God has made a better plan, that only in company with us should they reach their perfection, the perfection described in 1 Corinthians 15 as incorruptible, imperishable and immortal: *'These all died in faith, not having received the promises, but having seen them afar off were assured of them, embraced them and confessed that they were strangers and pilgrims on the earth.'* (Heb. 11:13)

The reason why God is not ashamed to be associated with them is because of their trust in His promises. In faith they left those things which they had in this life because they desired a better country, that is a heavenly country. The point is made again in v. 35: *'Others were tortured, not accepting deliverance, that they might obtain a better resurrection.'* *'A better resurrection'* must mean a resurrection to everlasting life rather than to shame and everlasting contempt (Dan.12:2).

Abel

The first character given as an example of faith is Abel. What was faithful about his sacrifice? His offering to God was taken from his flocks and was accepted, whereas Cain's was not. We assume they must both have been taught by their parents.

Embarrassing as it would have been for them, the way in which God had covered their nakedness was by the shedding of the blood of slain animals in order to clothe them with their skins. Abel understood the implication of this and had faith in the embryonic

Gospel of Salvation metaphorically shown in these things. This moved him to bring to God the pleasing offering. Having done the right thing and been commended for it, the anger of Cain was aroused to such fury as to plan the murder of his younger brother. So was enacted the parable; the seed of the serpent, that is Cain, struck the seed of the woman, represented by Abel, on the heel. Thus, Abel's shed blood still speaks. It spoke of the death of Jesus, in the far distant future as *'the Lamb of God who takes away the sin of the world!'* Although it was to be in the far distant future, there was the hope of the death of the serpent which had deceived Abel's parents; a deception that had brought the curse upon them and all their offspring. God testified that Abel's gifts were acceptable and were motivated by faith. Thus, his example speaks to future generations who want to please God.

We might observe that Cain's offering was of the fruits of the earth. Metaphorically, the earth is man. He was made out of it and the fruits of sinful, earthy nature could not lead to salvation. Paul describes it in the language of the A.V. *'The first man* [Adam] *is of the earth earthy'.* Such cannot inherit the kingdom of God as corruption cannot inherit incorruption.' (1 Cor. 15:47–50) Cain seemingly, either did not understand this, or rebelled on principle. So, he returned to the dust from whence he had come, to perish forever. Cain's lack of understanding, coupled with an unwillingness to learn, was copied by future generations which led to the wholesale corruption of the earth to such an extent that God became utterly disgusted with His creation and determined to destroy it.

Enoch

Genesis 5 says that Enoch lived 365 years, walking faithfully with God and then he was no more because God took him. Hebrews says that he did not experience death and that before God took him away, he was commended as one who pleased God. Verse 6 follows with the well-known lesson that *'without faith it is impossible to please Him, for he who comes to God must believe that He is, and that He is a rewarder of those who diligently seek*

Him.' (Heb 11:6). In its context this lesson must surely be a description of the pleasure Enoch gave to God.

Noah

Noah believed God when warned about the forthcoming destruction of all that breathed. Not only did he believe; he heeded God's instructions to prepare an ark for the saving of his family. We read the account in a few minutes, but Noah gave up his normal life to construct a huge vessel. It probably took 120 years of heavy labour, but it saved his family from an event which had never been seen before. We imagine the vessel being constructed far away from the sea so that ordinary people would scoff at what appeared to be a vast folly. The faith of Noah was evident over decades as he felled hundreds of trees, converted them into planks and ribs, fixing them by some means, waterproofing the huge hull and fitting it out. It was a monumental feat demanding an unfaltering faith over a very long period of time. Only after God closed him in and shut the door and the rains fell and floods began to appear was his faith vindicated. All but the eight souls consisting of Noah and his family perished in the flood, which no one else believed would ever happen!

We should not forget that in all probability, Noah and his family must surely have been bereaved of many of their relations and neighbours. Noah had many brothers and sisters, children of his father Lamech. His wife, and his daughters-in-law would all have been bereaved, as well as suffering the mockery aimed at the family due to Noah's seemingly insane persistence in such an unbelievable folly.

In our insignificant way we have been preaching the end of the world as promised in the word of God and that to escape extinction one must believe the Gospel and be baptised into Christ. We know that we are thought to be foolish people because we believe the Bible to be true. We are confident that our faith will also be vindicated in the end. That too, is a manifestation of our faith even though insignificant compared to Noah's.

Peter writes that God waited patiently for Noah to finish the ark in order that he might be saved from the waters of the flood. All with him were brought to safety through the waters, which he likens to baptism. The water prefigured baptism through which we are now brought to safety. He adds, baptism is not the washing away of bodily pollution, but the appeal made to God by a good conscience. It brings salvation through the resurrection of Jesus Christ. (1 Peter 3:20–21) In other words, faith is shown to exist by baptism, the appeal made to God of a good conscience; faith and works working together, as James puts it.

Abraham

The next example is so important that it occupies twelve out of the forty verses in this chapter. It is about Abraham and Sarah. Abraham was spoken of by those Pharisees antagonistic to Jesus as "our father Abraham." For Jewish Christians hesitating about clinging to Jesus instead of returning to Judaism, Abraham was a key example. Abraham is named seventy-five times in the New Testament. He is important to the teaching about justification by faith.

> *'By faith Abraham, when he was tested, offered up Isaac, and he who had received the promises offered up his only begotten son, of whom it was said, "In Isaac your seed shall be called," concluding that God was able to raise him up, even from the dead, from which he also received him in a figurative sense.'* (Heb 11:17-19)

This is a clear type of the birth, death and resurrection of Jesus. Jesus is unique in being the only begotten Son of God. His birth had nothing to do with a man. He was born of the woman and begotten by God. Sarah was a type of this unique begettal inasmuch as she was barren and had no child, yet God miraculously gave her a son in her old age (Gen 21:1–2). Jesus was slain according to the will of his Father and raised again to glory and immortality. Surely this was what Jesus meant when he said: *'Your father Abraham rejoiced to see my day, and he saw it and was glad.'* (John 8:56)

This example is truly remarkable. Abraham had waited 25 years for this son. Isaac was presumably an adolescent at least, when this dreadful test of faith fell upon his father. Some think Isaac could have been about thirty years old; in either case, Isaac must have cooperated with his father by offering no resistance. It is easy to imagine Abraham's joy when his hand was stayed and his eyes were directed to the ram caught in the thicket.

Paul's inspired comment on the astonishing faith of Abraham sums up his example. God had said before he had any descendants: *'You will be the father of many nations.'* That hope looked hopeless due to the ages of himself and Sarah, yet he never doubted God's promise. On the contrary, he honoured God by his firm conviction that He was able to perform what He had promised. It is for that reason that God counted him righteous (Rom 4:16–22). So, in believing in the promises, he reasoned that God would raise Isaac from the dead, just as he himself must rise to life everlasting to inherit the everlasting promises.

We must try to develop a similar attitude of trust as that shown by Abraham? As Paul wrote: *'flesh and blood cannot inherit the kingdom of God; nor does corruption inherit incorruption.'* (1 Cor. 15:50) God's kingdom is eternal and so we must be brought from death to life and changed from mortality to immortality. God will give us the victory over death through Jesus Christ our Lord. Therefore we must stand firm and immovable in that conviction.

Isaac, Jacob and Joseph

Isaac, Jacob and Joseph are the next examples of faith about which very little is said. Although Genesis has much to say about them and their faith, Paul only mentions that at the end of their lives, they remained convinced of the promises of God.

He mentions Isaac's blessing of Jacob as an example of his faith, although the Genesis record seems to imply that it was a somewhat faltering faith at that time.

In Jacob's case, the example of faith chosen concerns his blessing of Joseph's sons shortly before his death. Joseph, for all his amazing life in service to God, is commended for his faith in mentioning the departure of the Children of Israel, and his instructions concerning his bones. He had ruled Egypt for eighty years with all its distractions, but never forgot the promises of God.

Amram and Jochebed

Exodus 2:2 says that the mother of Moses hid her new-born child three months because he was a beautiful child. Hebrews 11:23 mentions the same fact, adding that they were not afraid of the king's commandment. Acts 7:20 confirms that the baby remained in his father's house three months and was then placed in the basket in the river.

It is intriguing that the Hebrew midwives were not afraid of the king either, disregarding his murderous command to destroy all male babies born to Hebrew women. We do not know what was so special about the child, but something about him attracted Pharaoh's daughter to adopt him, presumably with the consent of her father. He was brought up as an Egyptian prince.

Surely, God's covenant with Abraham that his descendants would be strangers or sojourners in a land not theirs for 400 years was remembered by Moses' parents. Moses' birth was about 50 years after the death of Joseph who knew and believed that God would take the Children of Israel back to the Promised Land.

Exodus 6 and 1 Chronicles 6 both record that Amram was the grandson of Levi through Kohath, which implies that Moses was the fourth generation. Also, as in the case of Abraham, a generation separated Amram from Jochebed in that he married his father's sister. Jochebed means 'Yah is honour' or 'the glory of Yah'

Moses

Moses' parents form a bridge to the next highly relevant example. It was to Moses that the Law was given, the very Law which was now obsolete and which the scribes and Pharisees pretended to follow so punctiliously. In fact, they had lost sight of the Law through their academic traditions. So, how significant are the facts given about Moses? Firstly, all the recorded facts describe his faith and secondly, describe events in his life before the giving of the Law. The facts are these: he refused to be counted the son of Pharaoh's daughter, preferring to be associated with his own people. So, he rejected the pleasures and luxury of the Egyptian court: *'esteeming the reproach of Christ greater riches than the treasures in Egypt; for he looked to the reward.'* (Heb. 11:26) This is the characteristic of all the examples in chapter 11.

He must have learned of this reward from family history, which he later recorded in the first of the books of Moses. He must have understood the work of 'the seed of the woman' to which the promises to Abraham were added, that is the blessing through Abraham and his seed and the everlasting inheritance of the land of Canaan. To these were added the blessings of Jacob concerning his sons, especially those to Judah and Joseph. He would have been taught the amazing facts about Joseph's life, how in God's providence he became the saviour of the world. All of these we assume had been instilled into him by his faithful parents in the brief years before he was handed over to Pharaoh's daughter. We recall that his mother was appointed to be his nurse. His faith in those promises of God far outweighed in his mind the attractions of Egypt.

Would Moses have spoken about his beliefs in the court of Pharaoh? If so, it would not be surprising if he was mocked and reproached for what looked like absurd hopes. The people to whom these promises were made were slaves and the promises were made nearly 400 years before, with no sign of fulfilment. In the eyes of the worldly court of Pharoah Moses seemed to be throwing away a glittering career in Egypt for what looked like a hopeless dream. Is this what is meant by 'the reproach' of Egypt?

The word used in Hebrews 11:26 and translated 'reproach' carries the meaning of defamation. (see also Rom.15:3, Heb 10:33, 13:13)   In other words Moses would have been regarded as a poor deluded man, an object of ridicule.

Moses knew that the time was fast approaching when their return to the Promised Land should be expected. He was disappointed that his fellow Israelites were unaware of the facts as promised by God when He confirmed the covenant with Abraham. (Gen.15)

Hebrews does not mention the faith and courage needed in this humblest of men, to go repeatedly into the presence of Pharaoh to warn him about one devastating plague after another. Humanly speaking, Pharaoh had the power to summarily execute the troublesome Moses. But Moses did not fear the anger or threats of Pharaoh, because his trust in God was highly developed. He feared not who threatened him with death if he ever appeared before him again. Through faith, he kept the Passover, believing that the terrible plague, which would afflict the Egyptians so severely, would not affect any Israelite who obeyed God's command. Having received their instructions, the record says: *'So the people bowed their heads and worshiped. Then the children of Israel went away and did so; just as the LORD had commanded Moses and Aaron, so they did.'* (Exodus 12:27–28) We notice however, that the record says that he, Moses, kept the Passover, which infers that this was the inauguration of the feast in Egypt, celebrating Israel's redemption. Soon afterwards they were baptised into Moses in the sea. (1 Cor.10:2) The saving of every one of the firstborn of Israel on the night when every firstborn of Egypt, from Pharaoh down to the humblest servant girl and their cattle died was a type of God's plan of redemption. Like Abraham,

Moses understood the significance of all this as a type of redemption through the seed of the woman.

The Israelites

'By faith they passed through the Red Sea as by dry land, whereas the Egyptians, attempting to do so, were drowned.' (Heb. 11:29) This surely required considerable trust in God; a trust which was rewarded as the waters returned and inundated the pursuing Egyptian hosts. Pharaoh and his mighty army perished, but Israel were in figure, baptised in that same sea and were given the hope of the inheritance of the land promised to Abraham. The drowning of Pharoah and the Egyptian army in the sea brought into sharp focus that this was God's salvation of His people.

Everything mentioned in this chapter 11 so far, preceded the giving of the Law. Even so, much had been taught about salvation through Jesus Christ. For example, it shows that salvation would come through:

- the seed of the woman but not of man

- the seed promised to Abraham whose death was foreseen in the enacted parable of Isaac

- the seed who would share in the promises made to Abraham

Salvation through faith in God and Christ were all announced long before the Law. These examples should have been powerful in persuading the Hebrews not to turn away from salvation through faith in Christ, rather than returning to the Law which could not save them.

The examples of faith which follow are all after the giving of the Law. The first example concerns the next generation of Israelites after those who died in the wilderness. They had the faith to:

- cross the Jordan at the season in which it overflowed its banks

- they were circumcised on the Canaanite side of the river which disabled them for a few days when they were vulnerable to attack

- they entered the land which their fathers were too frightened to do

- they had faith to obey God's instructions which brought the walls of Jericho down.

Throughout the campaigns to take the land they saw the mighty hand of God in miracle after miracle. All of this was accomplished through faith, not by law.

A Gentile of faith

The next example is striking because it concerns a Gentile woman who had nothing to do with the Law. However, she was to be one of those 'from all nations' destined to be blessed through Abraham and his seed. We are of course referring to the harlot Rahab who did not perish when Jericho fell. Her declaration of faith in the God of Israel is remarkable: *'I know that the LORD has given you the land, that the terror of you has fallen on us, and that all the inhabitants of the land are fainthearted because of you. For we have heard how the LORD dried up the water of the Red Sea for you when you came out of Egypt, and what you did to the two kings of the Amorites who were on the other side of the Jordan, Sihon and Og, whom you utterly destroyed. And as soon as we heard these things, our hearts melted; neither did there remain any more courage in anyone because of you, for the LORD your God, He is God in heaven above and on earth beneath.'* (Josh. 2:9-11)

Her faith was manifested in beseeching the spies to save her and her family. Furthermore she carefully carried out their instructions for the salvation of her family. She could easily have quailed as the Israelites silently encircled the city day after day until the seventh day when everything changed. Then the Israelites went round the city seven times with the ram's horns sounding ominously. This was followed by the great shout when the walls fell flat, while her house on the wall remained standing. Her trust was absolutely vindicated. As James teaches, she proved her faith by her works. In God's lovingkindness, her life was transformed. She and all her family were saved from destruction; she became the wife of Salmon, the son of the leader of the tribe of Judah and their son was Boaz. One wonders whether she was still alive to see her son marry Ruth, the third Gentile woman in the ancestry of Jesus?

Other men and women of faith

'What more shall I say? For the time would fail me to tell of Gideon and Barak and Samson and Jephthah...' For in depth study of these four Judges see *The Gospel in the book of Judges* by Ian Giles. The list continues by referring to Samuel, the gift of God to Hannah, who in turn promised to give him to the LORD. He brought a degree of faithfulness to Israel.

David is the next one mentioned; he subdued kingdoms and administered justice and also received glorious promises. We can read the history of these men and women in the Old Testament, their humanity evident, but nonetheless reckoned faithful in God's sight

Then follows a list of experiences endured by others and we can identify some who fit the descriptions such as:

- the widow of Zarephath whose son was raised to life by Elijah

- the Shunamite woman whose son was raised by Elisha

- Shadrach, Meshach and Abed-Nego *'quenched the violence of fire'*

- Daniel *'stopped the mouths of lions'*

- Perhaps Joshua is referred to as the one who was *'made strong and became valiant in battle, turning to flight the armies of the aliens.'* Jehoshaphat and Hezekiah are others who could fit the description.

- One thinks of Micaiah the prophet who suffered mocking and imprisonment at the hand of Ahab and his false prophets.

God has seen fit to provide these many examples of what a living faith looks like. For us, who were once Gentiles and are now part of the Israel of God, chapter 11 is a favourite for its examples of faith. Indeed, we see ourselves as exceedingly privileged in that God has waited to include us in His promises:

> *'And all these, having obtained a good testimony through faith, did not receive the promise, God having provided something better for us, that they should not be made perfect apart from us.'* (Heb. 11:39–40)

May we have the good sense to hold fast to the wonderful hope, invisible as yet, but which our eyes have been opened to see through faith. May we not be so foolish as to despise the spirit of grace by which we shall be saved.

12 THE CHASTENING OF THE LORD

AN EXPOSITION OF HEBREWS CHAPTER 12

Paul was acutely conscious of the damage he had done to Jesus' brothers and sisters. He had been a 'high-flyer' among the Pharisees, one of those John called collectively 'antichrist'. These were the people who stirred up trouble wherever they could to destroy those of the Way. Acts 14:1–2 gives an example of how the Jews at Iconium stirred up the Gentiles, poisoning their minds against the Christians.

Saul of Tarsus was one of the most active in this persecution of the believers, breathing threats and murder against the disciples of the Lord. No wonder he wrote to Timothy about how very thankful he felt that Jesus had entrusted such a sinner to be his servant in spreading the Gospel which he had previously so violently opposed. *'I was once a blasphemer and a persecutor and a violent man, I was shown mercy because I acted in ignorance and unbelief'* admitted this highly educated Pharisee. He recognised that without the great mercy of the Lord, he would have been lost. He saw himself as the worst of sinners and therefore an example of the extent to which Jesus would go to save even such as him. (1 Tim 1:13–16).

Although we cannot be certain that Paul was the writer of this letter, his experience as a Pharisee, followed by his conversion would have made him an ideal apostle to persuade the Hebrews to hold fast to Jesus. The practical lessons which began at the end of chapter 10 and continued through chapter 11 come to a climax in chapter 12 with 'Therefore'.

The characteristics of faithful witnesses
'Therefore we also, since we are surrounded by so great a cloud of witnesses, let us lay aside every weight, and the sin which so easily ensnares us, and let us run with endurance the race that is

set before us.' (Heb. 12:1). The witnesses were those commended for their faith in Chapter 11. But, in what sense were they witnesses? The Greek word is *martur* from which the English word 'martyr' comes. A martyr is one who believes so strongly in God's promises that he is willing to die for them. The Hebrews would have known some brothers and sisters who had suffered imprisonment and death at the hand of Saul and his colleagues. They endured so much suffering because they strongly believed the promises to be true. That was how their faith was proved real. The faithful of each generation since have had those witnesses before them as examples to emulate; come what may, they believe in that 'better resurrection.'

The exhortation is, do not cumber yourselves with things which will weigh you down in the race for the reward. Whatever those encumbrances are, they are factors in our lives which make it harder to run the race. There are so many distractions in life which can cause a loss of focus on the reward. It is for each one of us to order our priorities so that we do not stumble in our running. Sin is mentioned as one of the stumbling blocks. So, the one unique man, unique because he did not sin, is brought to their and our attention as the climax and pinnacle of all the previous examples of faith.

Jesus, the author and finisher of our faith

'Looking unto Jesus, the author and finisher of our faith, who for the joy that was set before Him endured the cross, despising the shame, and has sat down at the right hand of the throne of God.' (Heb. 12:2) We notice that *'our'* as in *'our faith'* is not in the Greek text. The phrase is therefore *'looking unto Jesus, the author and finisher of faith.'* The faith of all generations of believers is perfected through Jesus. He is the foundation on which faith is built. We are made righteous or perfect through faith in him. This principle is explained in Romans 4:23–5:2, when Scripture recorded that Abraham's faith was counted to him as righteousness. *'The words "it was credited to him" were written not for him alone, but also for us, to whom God will credit*

righteousness—for us who believe in him who raised Jesus our Lord from the dead. He was delivered over to death for our sins and was raised to life for our justification.' (Rom 4:23-25 NIV). So, like Abraham we are able to rejoice in the hope of the glory of God.

If Christ had not died for our sins and been raised to life there would have been no foundation on which our faith could be built, so we could not be forgiven and made righteous! Take Jesus out of the picture and we become hopeless, because, if Jesus had not been raised we would still be unforgiven sinners with no hope of resurrection and transformation to the glory of God.

The greatest example of faith

Jesus had suffered at the hands of the same people who were now troubling the Hebrews. Jesus had endured humiliation and pain because he trusted his Father absolutely, believed in the promised reward and looked forward to the joy of it. That joy had come when he had been raised to an altogether better life, now possessing divine nature and seated at the right hand of the throne of God! To all that, must be added the joy of knowing that he had brought salvation to those he loved; the faithful of all ages, both Jews and Gentiles, those his Father had called and given to him. As Isaiah 53 said, after he had suffered, he would see the light of life and be satisfied with the knowledge that he would justify many.

The exhortation to the Jewish Christians to whom this letter is addressed was therefore to: *'Consider Him who endured such hostility from sinners against Himself, lest you become weary and discouraged in your souls. You have not yet resisted to bloodshed, striving against sin.'* (Heb. 12:3–4) Simeon had prophesied: *'Behold, this Child is destined for the fall and rising of many in Israel, and for a sign which will be spoken against... that the thoughts of many hearts may be revealed.'* (Luke 2:34) Indeed, the thoughts of many hearts had been revealed and found to be very hard.

Our Father's training

Some, such as Stephen and James had lost their lives. Others had been beaten and many had suffered brutally at the hands of Saul of Tarsus. Even so, an important principle had to be understood:

> *'You have forgotten the exhortation which speaks to you as to sons: "My son, do not despise the chastening of the Lord, nor be discouraged when you are rebuked by Him, for whom the Lord loves He chastens, and scourges every son whom He receives."'* (Heb. 12:5–6)

They may have heard how the apostles had been arrested and flogged and yet had left the presence of the council, rejoicing that they were counted worthy to suffer dishonour for the name. As James later wrote:

> *'My brethren, count it all joy when you fall into various trials, knowing that the testing of your faith produces patience. But let patience have its perfect work, that you may be perfect and complete, lacking nothing.'* (James 1:2–4)

The exhortation follows: *'If you endure chastening, God deals with you as with sons; for what son is there whom a father does not chasten?'* (Heb. 12:7)

What a privilege! God calls some to be His children but does not leave them to fare for themselves. On the contrary, He goes to great lengths to train, discipline and educate His sons and daughters. He prepares them thoroughly for eternal companionship with His beloved son Jesus and the possession of His kingdom. The history of Israel as set before us in Scripture is, that notwithstanding God's fatherly training, His children often rebelled against Him. As Hosea 6:4-7 says:

> *'O Ephraim, what shall I do to you? O Judah, what shall I do to you? For your faithfulness is like a morning cloud, and like the early dew it goes away. Therefore I have hewn them by the prophets, I have slain them by the words of My mouth; and your judgments are like light that goes forth. For I desire mercy and not sacrifice, and the knowledge of God more than burnt offerings. But like men they transgressed the covenant; there they dealt treacherously with Me.'*

We feel the hurt experienced by God as the Father of Israel when He said: *'I taught Ephraim to walk, taking them by their arms; but they did not know that I healed them. I drew them with gentle cords, with bands of love, and I was to them as those who take the yoke from their neck. I stooped and fed them.'* (Hos. 11:3–4) This was the child He loved and brought out of Egypt!

History shows that acknowledging God and loving Him steadfastly is not natural to human nature. We have been given great intelligence and abilities and freedom to choose how to use them. The lesson of all Scripture, beginning in Eden, is that human nature is much more likely to follow its own inclinations rather than the wisdom of our Father. This means that loving our Father requires constancy and concentration. It is not something to think about now and again, but should be kept in mind always. It means loving to read everything He says in His word, taking it seriously and responding to Him in prayer and doing what He says. Fundamentally, it means trusting Him as a small child trusts its father.

However, if you are not disciplined it is because you are not God's children. Moses speaking of Israel said: *'they are corrupt and not His children.'* (Deut. 32:5 NIV) Jesus told those who no longer believed in him but asserted that they were children of Abraham and not illegitimate, *'you are children of the your father the devil.'* Again in his parable of the sower, he spoke of the good seed being children of the kingdom and the weeds as the people of the evil one.

Proverbs chapter 1 rebukes those foolish people who refuse to heed wisdom. '... *How long will mockers delight in mockery and fools hate knowledge? Repent at my rebuke! Then I will pour out my thoughts to you, I will make known to you my teachings.'* (Prov.1:22–23 NIV) There are only two classes of people in this world; the seed of the serpent and the seed of the woman.

The exposition continues by saying that if we respected our natural father's discipline, a discipline which seemed best to him, how much more should we submit to the Father of spirits and live? The Father of spirits is our Creator, the Almighty who designed us and gives us life. His discipline is for our benefit, that we might partake of His holiness. Our heavenly Father is guiding us towards His image and likeness, the results of which will be seen when we are changed to immortality. Romans chapter 8 enlarges upon the transition from the mind of the flesh to the mind of God.

An amazing incentive

As Peter explains: *'His divine power has given to us all things that pertain to life and godliness, through the knowledge of Him who called us by glory and virtue, by which have been given to us exceedingly great and precious promises, that through these you may be partakers of the divine nature, having escaped the corruption that is in the world through lust.'* (2 Pet. 1:3–4)

Consider Jesus we were told in verse 3. He endured the hatred of the same men who were now trying to crush the faith of his disciples. Those to whom this letter is addressed were probably in the midst of a severe trial of faith. Would they accept it patiently as a case of the Father's discipline? Were they going to follow men who put our Lord Jesus to death, or follow the Father of the Lord Jesus? The right answer to that test may seem obvious to us with hindsight, but, in the heat of the moment, it may not have seemed so obvious. But as v. 11 says: *'no chastening seems to be joyful for the present, but painful.'*

We know from experience that defending the Truth against false brethren can be one of the toughest trials we ever have to face. It is what Jesus endured and Paul suffered it too. Most of Paul's letters were defending the Gospel of Christ against those who thought themselves righteous through their own works. Those self-righteous men were angry at being told that they were sinners just as all men were, both Jews and Gentiles! All were equally dependent on the grace and kindness of God. If only they would acknowledge the wisdom of the Father, the result would be: *'... the peaceable fruit of righteousness to those who have been trained by it.'*

If they would only recognise it, this reference was a powerful exhortation. It is the first of a series of exhortations taken from Moses and the prophets and may have come from Isaiah. In an appeal to the women of Jerusalem, Isaiah said: *'The work of righteousness will be peace, And the effect of righteousness, quietness and assurance forever. My people will dwell in a peaceful habitation, In secure dwellings, and in quiet resting places.'* (Isa. 32:17–18) Isaiah describes Israel as being like a desert, devoid of righteous fruit, until the spirit of the LORD is poured on them from on high. Then the desert becomes a fertile field, and the Lord's justice will then dwell in the desert, His righteousness will live in the fertile field.

Jesus is the one poured out on them from on high as Isa.11 says: *'There shall come forth a rod from the stem of Jesse, And a branch shall grow out of his roots. The spirit of the LORD shall rest upon Him, the spirit of wisdom and understanding, the spirit of counsel and might, the spirit of knowledge and of the fear of the LORD.'* (Isa. 11:1–2) The passage concludes with the wonderful picture: *'They shall not hurt nor destroy in all My holy mountain for the earth shall be full of the knowledge of the LORD as the waters cover the sea.'*

Peace is first peace with God. The faithful person ceases to be an enemy of God because he believes that God exists and is searching diligently for Him.

'Therefore strengthen the hands which hang down'

The next exhortation (Heb. 12:12) is also drawn from Isaiah: *'Therefore strengthen the hands which hang down, and the feeble knees, and make straight paths for your feet, so that what is lame may not be dislocated, but rather be healed.'*

Again, if they knew the context, this encouragement to return to Christ is also very powerful. The source is Isaiah 35:1-5. It begins with the metaphor of the desert again: *'The wilderness and the wasteland shall be glad for them, and the desert shall rejoice and blossom as the rose; It shall blossom abundantly and rejoice, even with joy and singing. The glory of Lebanon shall be given to it, the excellence of Carmel and Sharon. They shall see the glory of the* LORD, *the excellency of our God. Strengthen the weak hands, and make firm the feeble knees. Say to those who are fearful-hearted, "Be strong, do not fear! Behold, your God will come with vengeance, With the recompense of God; He will come and save you." Then the eyes of the blind shall be opened, And the ears of the deaf shall be unstopped.'* A wonderful day of salvation for the house of Jacob when God will intervene to enable them to know Him. (Isa. 6;9–10, Ezek. 36:24–32, Mat 13:15–19, John 12:40, Acts 28:26–27.)

Hebrews 12 continues like this: *'Pursue peace with all people, and holiness, without which no one will see the* LORD: *looking carefully lest anyone fall short of the grace of God; lest any root of bitterness springing up cause trouble, and by this many become defiled.'* (Heb.12:14–15)

Reading between the lines, the struggles between the Judaisers and the faithful brothers and sisters took place in their congregations and would have led to anything but peace. Paul refers to some people who were throwing the Galatian ecclesia

- 143 -

into confusion, trying to pervert the Gospel of Christ. The letter from the Jerusalem meeting to Antioch refers to the same problem. It would seem that the Judaisers were in fact false brethren infiltrating the meetings to wreak havoc from within. The Jerusalem meeting may have been particularly vulnerable to such deceitful tactics, Jerusalem being the centre of Judaism with the Temple, Sanhedrin, palace of the High Priest and where Pharisees and Sadducees congregated

A Root of bitterness

We know that at times we can disturb the peace of the meeting by being intolerant of things that do not conform to our opinion as to what is decent and orderly. Paul makes it very clear that we must not impose our opinions on others. We are not of course referring to scriptural principles. In another context to do with food, Paul wrote: *'Therefore let us pursue the things which make for peace and the things by which one may edify another. Do not destroy the work of God for the sake of food. All things indeed are pure, but it is evil for the man who eats with offence. It is good neither to eat meat nor drink wine nor do anything by which your brother stumbles or is offended or is made weak.'* (Rom. 14:19–22)

Here Paul was advising an ecclesia in Rome, consisting of Jewish and Gentile brothers, but the Jerusalem meeting was warned like this: *'lest any root of bitterness springing up cause trouble, and by this many become defiled.'* The exhortation was particularly potent because again it comes from Moses.

'... and you saw their abominations and their idols which were among them—wood and stone and silver and gold); so that there may not be among you man or woman or family or tribe, whose heart turns away today from the LORD our God, to go and serve the gods of these nations, and that there may not be among you a root bearing bitterness or wormwood; and so it may not happen, when he hears the words of this curse, that he blesses himself in his heart, saying, 'I shall have peace, even though I follow the

dictates of my heart'—as though the drunkard could be included with the sober.' (Deut. 29:17–19)

Such were to be put to death. Of course, it appears harsh to 21st century liberal opinion which pretends to include and tolerate every whim and vice of human nature. But, if Israel had done as Moses commanded, countless Israelites would have have been saved from corrupting their way and perishing as a consequence.

Treating God's promises lightly

The next lesson is about the profanity of holding God's promises lightly. This is a very sharp point indeed. Esau was so careless about the privilege due to the firstborn son that he exchanged the birthright for a morsel, a moment of self-gratification (Heb. 12:16–17). However, when the time came for Isaac to bestow the blessings upon his sons and Rebecca had manipulated matters to ensure that Jacob received the blessing of the first born, it was too late. There could be only one first born to receive the blessing and Isaac had given it to Jacob. Jacob had acquired it from Esau by agreement, but he and his mother so much desired it as to collude in the deception of Isaac. They sought to ensure that God's message to Rebekah about her twin sons was not overlooked. *'The older shall serve the younger'* was what God had decreed.

Above all, Jacob and Rebecca both esteemed the promises to be of the greatest importance and not to be held lightly. Esau's tears were clearly not because he regretted his cavalier attitude to the blessing, but because he sought to persuade his father to revise his blessings to his advantage. Esau never showed any remorse for his profane carelessness over the promises of God to his father and grandfather. Jacob and his mother valued the promises so much that they were willing to risk deception to achieve their goal.

The Hebrews therefore, should realise that in turning back to the Law for the short term advantages that might come from joining the Judaisers, they would be just like the profane Esau. They would be rejecting God's gracious offer of salvation and turning away from the love of Jesus who gave his life to save them. In effect, they were treading the Son of God under foot. This was an extremely serious point which found its mark and arrested their turning away from Christ to the law.

The climax of the appeal

These verses rehearse Israel's experience at Sinai. So terrifying was it that they begged Moses to ask God never speak to them again. God graciously agreed to their request and Moses reported back to them. The LORD would give them a prophet and put all His words into his mouth. He would tell them everything which the LORD commanded them, but beware, God will hold to account those that do not listen. During Jesus' ministry people listening to his teaching queried whether he was that prophet. It should have been obvious that he was by his claim to speak only the words God gave him to speak; in addition the mighty works which God did by him testified to his authority. After healing the lame man Peter reminded them of the prophet like to Moses with the stern warning, if you do not listen to him you will be utterly destroyed (Acts 3:22–23). Stephen addressing the Sanhedrin fearlessly accused them of betraying and murdering the righteous one. How stubborn they were, pagan at heart and deaf to the truth. Just as they had thrust Moses aside, so did they to 'the prophet like unto Moses'. In their fury, they treated Stephen as they had all God's messengers and utter destruction awaited them.

Paul now introduces a profound contrast which ought, if nothing else, to change their minds. They had not come to the terror of Sinai. They had been baptised into Christ Jesus and had come to Mount Zion, to joy and wonderful things. (vv. 22-24):

> 'But you have come to Mount Zion and to the city of the living God, the heavenly Jerusalem, to an innumerable company of angels, to the general assembly and church of the firstborn who are registered in heaven, to God the Judge of all, to the spirits of just men made perfect, to Jesus the Mediator of the New Covenant, and to the

blood of sprinkling that speaks better things than that of Abel.'

This is a long and intense sentence which is rich in metaphors. What is it saying?

What was the distinction between Zion and Sinai? Paul explained this allegory in his letter to the Galatians. Mount Sinai stood for Hagar the bondwoman. Her children would be born into slavery. Sinai stood for Jerusalem of today, for she and her children are in slavery. By slavery he meant the law given at Sinai. But Christian Jews should have left all that behind when they had put on Christ. They had been freed from slavery and become children of Abraham's wife Sarah. Sarah was not subject to the Law. She stood for the heavenly Jerusalem, Zion, the city of God. (Gal.4:21–27)

Why would anybody in their right mind choose to return to slavery after being made free? The blessings attached to being brothers and sisters of Christ are astounding. Jesus promised: *'Behold, I am coming quickly! Hold fast what you have, that no one may take your crown. He who overcomes, I will make him a pillar in the temple of My God, and he shall go out no more. I will write on him the name of My God and the name of the city of My God, the New Jerusalem, which comes down out of heaven from My God. And I will write on him My new name.'* (Rev. 3:11–12)

That city is described in some detail in Revelation 21 and is amplified by another figure, the bride, the Lamb's wife. So, why would one who had known the freedom brought through Christ and its glorious heavenly promises prefer the bondage associated with the earthly Jerusalem?

An innumerable company of angels

A follower of Jesus had also come *'to an innumerable company of angels.'* Were they not the ministering spirits of Hebrews 1:14 sent to serve those who will inherit salvation? Would the angels not be joyful at the success of their work? They could also have remembered the innumerable company of angels of Revelation 5:11 singing in praise of the Lamb who was slain and was worthy to receive power, wealth, wisdom, strength, glory and praise. (There is a case for believing that Revelation was already in circulation at the time Hebrews was written.) Did not Jesus say: *'There will be more joy in heaven over one sinner who repents than over ninety-nine righteous persons who need no repentance.'* (Luke 15:7) Those who despised and executed Jesus were the ones who thought they had no need of repentance as they were meticulously and slavishly keeping the Law, which kept them in bondage to it.

The church of the firstborn

The next phrase in that intense sentence is *'to the general assembly and church of the firstborn who are registered in heaven.'* This is a reference back to Hebrews 3:6: *'but Christ is faithful over God's house as a son.'* The contrast is between a son and a servant. Moses was a servant in God's house whereas Jesus is the son of the house. The believers belong to that house on condition that they hold fast to the great hope of salvation through Christ. This the family of God; they were His children who did not lose their faith in the head of the house, but held fast to the great hope to the end. Their names are registered in heaven, recorded in the book of life. *'He who overcomes shall be clothed in white garments, and I will not blot out his name from the Book of Life; but I will confess his name before my Father and before His angels.'* (Rev. 3:5)   To leave that house of God and His son with all its present and future blessings would be folly indeed.

God the Judge of all

The great appeal continues to a crescendo: *'to God the Judge of all.'* God had given the law, and its purpose had been achieved. God had sent forth His son, born under the law, to redeem those under the law so that they might receive the adoption as sons. Therefore, they were no longer slaves but sons. The law was thus made obsolete; it was God's decision as the judge of all men. Woe betide those who rejected His son whom the law had foreseen in so many shadowy figures.

The complex sentence continues: *'... to the spirits of just men made perfect.'* Here, the contrast is made between those in bondage to the law and its many sacrifices for sin and the freedom from all that, because forgiveness was now given to those in Christ. They had been made perfect by the grace of God and had joined all those characters who had been counted righteous through faith.

Jesus the Mediator of the New Covenant

The long sentence ends by saying that they had come, not only to all the wonderful things already mentioned but *'to Jesus the Mediator of the New Covenant, and to the blood of sprinkling that speaks better things than that of Abel.'* The features of the New Covenant have already been explained in this letter, but its advantages were so great in comparison to the law. That law is called the Old Covenant which was written on tablets of stone. The New Covenant said this: *'I will put My law in their minds, and write it on their hearts; and I will be their God, and they shall be My people.'* (Jer. 31:33) *'My law'* is so uncomplicated and easily written in the mind and heart. Love the Lord God with all your being and love your neighbour as yourself. God's word shows how to do these things with an abundance of illustrations.

That wonderful New Covenant was confirmed by the blood of Jesus as the covenant victim; he is the one the Hebrews had once joyfully come to, but were in danger of deserting. His blood is indeed better by far than that of Abel's sacrifice. Abel was an imperfect man trying to please God by offering a sacrifice which could not make him perfect. Nonetheless, it was offered in faith and looked forward to the blood of Christ which would make him perfect.

Do not refuse Him that speaks from heaven

Now Paul is coming to the nub of the matter; see to it that you do not refuse to listen to the LORD who speaks from heaven. You know what befell those who turned deaf ears to that great voice. From Adam onwards the voice has put on record the consequence of such arrogance. Those who gave no heed to Moses, who spoke God's word to them, died in the wilderness. Sennacharib, who lifted up his insolent eyes against the Holy One of Israel, fled to his own land leaving behind 185,000 warriors dead outside Jerusalem. Now it was Jesus' turn. He had spoken so plainly the words of his Father, but had been despised and rejected and murdered by the Jewish authorities. They could expect a mighty shaking and find that side of God's character which is a devouring fire. Instead of such a fearful end, give thanks that God has an unshakeable kingdom in view for those worship Him as He would be worshipped, with reverence and awe.

Let us have grace

Many translations render v. 28 *'let us have grace'* as let us 'be thankful' or 'grateful'. This is a legitimate translation of the Greek *charis* and certainly should be the response of a true believer. However, in the context of this letter it might be better understood as, 'let us receive forgiveness of sins (or the gift of righteousness)'. These blessings are offered in the New Covenant through which the believer could receive an unshakeable kingdom. The Judaisers are trying to delude you into returning to the law which has been shaken and made obsolete, because it could not forgive your sins or bring you to an unshakeable kingdom. Indeed the kingdom of Israel had long before been shaken and overturned, and the relics of it were very soon to fall before the Romans, with its people being scattered far and wide among the Gentiles.

13 PRACTICAL EXHORTATIONS

AN EXPOSITION OF HEBREWS CHAPTER 13

The letter now focusses on practical exhortation typical of Paul's letters. Faith should have an effect on the believer's character and behaviour. As James wrote: *'For as the body without the spirit is dead, so faith without works is dead also.'* So, Paul urged *'Let brotherly love continue.'* Brotherly love is that love for Jesus as the head of the family and for his many brothers and sisters. Jesus laid down his life for you, and so the exhortation is that you should do the same for his family. Do not follow those false brethren who, with hate in their hearts for Jesus, were seeking to destroy God's family.

Show hospitality

The exhortations continue: *'Do not neglect to show hospitality to strangers, for thereby some have entertained angels unawares.'* This is a laudable characteristic, but it was more significant than it seems at first sight. It was a nudge to recall Abraham and his courtesy and hospitality to the three men who were passing by his camp at Mamre. He hastened to look after them, not knowing them to be angels on their way to the cities of the plain. Had they been allowed to pass by unnoticed he would not have heard God's promise that Sarah should have a son. Old though they both were, *'Is anything too hard for the LORD?'* was the stranger's lesson to the doubtful Sarah. Paul had previously written: *'By faith Sarah herself also received strength to conceive seed, and she bore a child when she was past age, because she judged Him faithful who had promised.'* It was a miracle which might prompt them to think of Jesus' miraculous birth and resurrection? Facts which Judaisers were desperately wanting to ignore, as Jews have done ever since.

But was Paul also alluding to the Gentile believers? The Jewish believers were accustomed to the laws of the temple precincts which put up a barrier to prevent strangers or Gentiles from approaching the temple. Now they were mixing with Gentiles and sharing the breaking of bread as members of the same family in Christ. Going back to the Law would result in them reverting to the old way of regarding all Gentiles as unclean, even refusing to sit down to eat with them. Abraham, long before the Law, eagerly entertained strangers.

Remember those in prison

'Remember those who are in prison, as though in prison with them, and those who are mistreated, since you also are in the body.' (Heb. 13:3 ESV) That last phrase is saying you are part of the one body in Christ. This verse implies that the Jewish authorities were still persecuting those of 'The Way,' just as Paul had done with terrifying zeal. In his defence before Agrippa, while suffering imprisonment brought about by those haters of Jesus, he said: *'I myself thought I must do many things contrary to the name of Jesus of Nazareth. This I also did in Jerusalem, and many of the saints I shut up in prison, having received authority from the chief priests; and when they were put to death, I cast my vote against them. And I punished them often in every synagogue and compelled them to blaspheme; and being exceedingly enraged against them, I persecuted them even to foreign cities.'* (Acts 26:9–11)

This exhortation to remember those who were suffering imprisonment would have been very close to Paul's heart. Many had visited him in various prisons and cared for him and he never ceased to be grateful for such ministrations. Among them were Luke, Timothy, Aristarchus, Tychicus, Onesimus, Mark, Demas and many more unnamed. The words of Jesus spring to mind: *'For I was hungry and you gave me food, I was thirsty and you gave me drink, I was a stranger and you welcomed me, I was naked and you clothed me, I was sick and you visited me, I was in prison and you came to me.'* (Matt. 25:35–36)

Most of us are unfamiliar with the harsh reality of hunger, homelessness, being clad in rags, cold and lonely. For the Christians, imprisonment came not as punishment for crime but for being followers of Jesus. The exhortation to remember those in prison was practical and necessary.

Marriage is honourable

'Marriage is honourable among all, and the bed undefiled; but fornicators and adulterers God will judge.' (Heb.13:4) Such an exhortation was as necessary then as it is now. Such infidelity cannot be hidden from God and He will judge. When David sinned against God in the matter of Bathsheba and Uriah, God said that David had despised Him. Thus, David had lapsed in his love for God, distracted by lust. Deliberately disobeying God's instructions is to despise Him. Every Jew would have known the Ten Commandments which formed the covenant made by God at Mount Sinai, just as those commandments were well known in western society at one time. Such moral guidance was foreign to Greek and Roman societies just as it has become in western societies today.

Be content with what you have

'Let your conduct be without covetousness; be content with such things as you have. For He Himself has said, "I will never leave you nor forsake you." So we may boldly say: "The Lord is my helper, I will not fear what man can do to me."' (Heb. 13:5–6)

This exhortation teaches all God's servants to put their trust in the LORD, to depend on Him, rather than adopt the common attitude of mankind which is to be independent. However, it was especially meaningful to the Hebrews because it is a quotation from the last words of Moses (Deut. 31). There he exhorted Joshua and Israel to understand that God would go before them in the conquest of the land, and that He would never leave them. Therefore, they had every reason to be courageous and strong. What could man do to them with the Almighty leading the way? But Achan's covetousness at Jericho would come to remembrance with a jolt because it so marred the first two battles in the conquest of the land. God brought the walls of Jericho down in a moment, thus saving a long and difficult siege of the first of those cities that were *'walled up to heaven.'* The consequence of covetousness was the defeat at Ai. This came as a severe shock for it seemed as if God had forsaken them. In reality, it was a sharp lesson to all Israel who had refused to heed Moses' instructions concerning what was to be devoted to God.

The lesson spelt out in Hebrews 12:25–28 is that any who disregard God's commands are in jeopardy of being excluded from the *'the kingdom which cannot be shaken'*. The passage exhorts us to be thankful that we hope in such a kingdom and to worship God acceptably with reverence and godly fear. Moses warned: *'For our God is a consuming fire.'* (Deut. 4:24) and that He is *'a jealous God.'* This does not mean that we should be fearful of our God, for John says that *'perfect love should cast out fear'*. But we ought to treat our God with the utmost reverence and marvel that He has revealed Himself through His word. It absolutely rules out tampering with it or disregarding it to make it say something which suits us. Rather, as Psalm 119:11 says: *'Your word I have hidden in my heart that I might not sin against you.'*

The Lord is my helper

'The Lord is my helper; I will not fear. What can man do to me?' (Heb. 13:6). The Lord has indeed helped by taking the law away and replacing it with the two greatest commandments. They are easy to understand, unlike the Law of Moses with its complex laws which were difficult to remember and obey, and must often have been exasperating. Imagine being touched by an unclean flying insect, or picking up a carcase of one; your day is immediately disrupted by the command to wash your clothes and be unclean until evening. If an unclean creature such as a dead lizard fell into a clay pot, the pot and its contents became unclean and the pot had to be broken. It might have contained the family supper!

How much easier to understand and obey are those two greatest commands that Jesus identified in response to the lawyer's question. *'Jesus said to him, "You shall love the LORD your God with all your heart, with all your soul, and with all your mind. This is the first and great commandment. And the second is like it: You shall love your neighbour as yourself."'* (Matt 22:37-39) So, we can confidently say, 'The Lord is my helper; I will not fear; what can man do to me?'

Remember those who rule over you

'Remember those who rule over you, who have spoken the word of God to you, whose faith follow, considering the outcome of their conduct.' (Heb. 13:7) The readers of the epistle were instructed to remember the apostles who had been with Jesus during his ministry, but who had fled when Jesus was arrested. They had been utterly changed by the resurrection of Jesus and had received the spirit which changed unlearned men into expositors of the Scriptures. They would recall Stephen's faithful defence before the Sanhedrin and his horrible death by stoning. They would think of James, killed by Herod for political reasons. These men were their leaders and the exhortation is repeated in v. 17: *'Obey those who rule over you, and be submissive, for they watch out for your souls, as those who must give account. Let them do so with joy and not with grief, for that would be unprofitable for you.'*

The implication is that their leaders were having a difficult time with some of the recipients of the epistle. But returning to v. 8, the assurance is given that *'Jesus Christ is the same yesterday, today, and forever.'* The Greek here is quite emphatic: *'Jesus Christ is yesterday and today the same, and forever.'* Because Jesus is the same now, he is just as aware of their trials as he was of those experienced by the fathers.

Paul in earlier life as Saul, heard Jesus say that in persecuting his brothers he was persecuting Jesus himself. Jesus also wrote to the seven churches acknowledging the sufferings of some of them due to persecution and imprisonment and urged them to endure and not grow weary.

Verse 9 continues: *'Do not be carried about with various and strange doctrines. For it is good that the heart be established by grace, not with foods which have not profited those who have been occupied with them.'* Those *'various and strange doctrines'* refer to the Law with its complex regulations about food and much more besides. The heart was not strengthened by such things; it did not benefit those devoted to them. In contrast, the gift of righteousness or forgiveness through Jesus lightened the heart.

But what were the diverse strange teachings that were being circulated among them? We speculate that they may have been the continued adherence to the Law in matters such as fellowship offerings and the keeping of the feasts, practices which foreshadowed the Lord Jesus. But there was no point in them now that Jesus was with them, the embodiment of all that the Law foresaw. Why persist in the practices of the Law when Jesus had rendered them completely obsolete? Furthermore, such practices were exclusive to Jews and so brought division between Jews and Gentiles in the ecclesia.

We have an altar

'We have an altar from which those who serve the tabernacle have no right to eat.' (Heb. 13:10) The priests ministering the offerings, participated by being allotted a share of the food offered on the altar of the tabernacle. But the altar upon which Christ was offered was not that altar nor was it a Levitical priest who offered it. The lesson is taught in the procedures of the Day of Atonement. As Romans 3:25 (NIV) says: *'God presented Christ as a sacrifice of atonement, through the shedding of his blood – to be received by faith.'* No priest was involved. It was God who made the sacrifice!

Verse 11 continues: *'For the bodies of those animals, whose blood is brought into the sanctuary by the high priest for sin, are burned outside the camp.'* The blood of the sacrifice was presented by the High Priest by sprinkling it over the ark of the covenant. This was done on the one day in the year in which he was commanded to enter the Most Holy to obtain forgiveness for himself and all the people. We have already been told that the reality, as opposed to the shadow, is that Jesus entered into heaven itself with his own blood once and for all time. If some persisted in seeking atonement through the Levitical priests who were still ministering in the Temple, did it not show that they despised Jesus' sacrifice as being ineffectual? It showed a lack of faith in the great High Priest, who was seated at the right hand of God in the true house of God in the heavens. The gift of righteousness through faith was inevitably denied to such double minded persons. The exhortation which follows is imperative: *'let us go forth to Him, outside the camp.'*

Outside the camp

But, just as in the type of the Day of Atonement, the sacrificial body was not burnt on the altar but was carried outside the camp, so Jesus suffered outside the gate in order to sanctify the people through his own blood. Jesus was not slain in the temple in Jerusalem with all its association with the Law, but outside the city gate at the place for the execution of criminals. *'Therefore, Jesus also, that He might sanctify the people with His own blood, suffered outside the gate.'* (Heb.13:12) Thus he exhorted them to have nothing to do with the Temple, the priesthood of mortal men and the law they administered. Leave all that, and go out to Jesus who bore our sins and the disgrace of a condemned criminal, despised and rejected of men.

Furthermore, Jerusalem of the Sanhedrin, of the scribes and Pharisees is not the city you are to inherit, (vv. 13–14): *'Therefore let us go forth to Him, outside the camp, bearing his reproach.' For here we have no continuing city, but we seek the one to come.'* That is the heavenly Jerusalem spoken of in Hebrews 12:22 and Revelation 21.

The fruit of our lips

'Therefore, by Him let us continually offer the sacrifice of praise to God, that is, the fruit of our lips, giving thanks to His name.' (Heb. 13:15) Or, as the Psalmist said: *'Whoever offers praise glorifies Me; And to him who orders his conduct aright I will show the salvation of God.'* (Ps. 50:23) Isaiah 57:19 speaks of God creating praise on their lips by comforting and healing His people who mourned in Israel. *'Peace, peace, to those far and near… and I will heal them.'* Peter quoted these words on the day of Pentecost. In Hosea there is another wonderful passage: *'Return, Israel, to the LORD your God, your sins have been your downfall! Take words with you and return to the LORD. Say to him: "Forgive all our sins and receive us graciously, that we may offer the fruit of our lips."'* (Hos. 14:1–3 NIV) For those He has called, God has done everything to enable them to be saved. The better we understand this, the more we will be moved to praise Him, not only in words but in actions, thus giving glory to Him.

Sacrifices pleasing to God

'Do not neglect to do good and to share what you have, for such sacrifices are pleasing to God.' (Heb. 13:16 ESV) This exhortation is amplified in Paul's letter to the Romans where he besought the ecclesia to present themselves as living sacrifices. To do this meant changing their way of life, by ceasing to conform to the normal practices of society around them and following the mind of God. No longer would they selfishly serve only themselves, but would look out for others in need of their love and ministrations. To know that God is pleased with such who have tried to renew their minds, to be like Him, was extremely encouraging and far removed from the formal sacrifices made under the Law.

Paul's personal request

'Pray for us, for we are sure that we have a clear conscience, desiring to act honourably in all things. I urge you the more earnestly to do this in order that I may be restored to you the sooner.' (Heb. 13:18–19 ESV) In what sense should we understand *'Restored to you'*? Did Paul mean in the sense of

reinstating their relationship as it was before the upset? Or does he mean being able to visit them in Jerusalem? Perhaps he was asking for their prayers that both requests might be granted. They would have remembered with horror how Paul had been suddenly snatched out of the hands of the murderous crowd in the temple precincts and detained from that moment on by the Roman authorities. He was imprisoned for two years in Caesarea and a further two years in Rome. His second letter to Timothy written from Rome seems to imply that he anticipated the end of his life: *'I am already being poured out as a drink offering, and the time of my departure has come. I have fought the good fight, I have finished the race, I have kept the faith.'* (2 Tim. 4:6–7)

Paul's prayer for the Hebrews

'Now may the God of peace who brought up our Lord Jesus from the dead, that great Shepherd of the sheep, through the blood of the everlasting covenant, make you complete in every good work to do His will, working in you what is well pleasing in His sight, through Jesus Christ, to whom be glory forever and ever. Amen.' (Heb. 13:20–21) 'The God of peace' is a most evocative phrase reminding the readers of the extreme lovingkindness of the Father. He, the one offended by man's blasphemy in not trusting Him nonetheless, sought reconciliation in order to save the offender and bring peace. Romans 5:1–2 says: *'Therefore, having been justified by faith, we have peace with God through our Lord Jesus Christ, through whom also we have access by faith into this grace in which we stand, and rejoice in hope of the glory of God.'* This peace was brought about by God by raising Jesus from the dead, enabling him to carry out his priestly role of intercession for the faults of his brothers and sisters on condition that they believed.

The phrase, *'that great shepherd of the sheep',* is also a wonderful description of Jesus' character. Jesus depicted himself as a shepherd who was prepared to die for his sheep. In the past, so many shepherds of God's flock had neglected their duty and caused the leaderless flock to be lost. It was to those lost sheep that Jesus was sent, to gather them into his Father's fold. As Isaiah so beautifully expressed it: *'He will feed His flock like a shepherd; He will gather the lambs with His arm, and carry them in His bosom, and gently lead those who are with young.'* (Isa. 40:11)

These sentiments resonate with Psalm 78:70–72 where David is likewise so tenderly described. But Isaiah 63:11 might have impressed the Hebrews powerfully. It speaks of the kindness of the LORD and His great deeds done for His people, even though they rebelled and grieved His Holy Spirit. The prophet continues by asking: *'Where is he who brought them through the sea with the shepherd of his flock? Where is he who set His Holy Spirit among them, who sent his glorious arm of power to be at Moses' right hand, who divided the waters before them... This is how you guided your people to make for yourself a glorious name.'* (Isa. 63:11–14)

Moses and God's people were brought up out of the sea having been baptised in it and given newness of life, a resurrection which should have ended with rest in the kingdom of God. All this prefigured the death and resurrection of Jesus and all those who believed in him. The Hebrews had been baptised into Christ and should be heading for the kingdom of God. Surely, they were not going to fall in the wilderness and fail to enter that glorious rest.

The blood of the everlasting covenant

In the context of this letter, the blood of the everlasting covenant, refers to the New Covenant ratified by the blood of Jesus' sacrifice. However, it has also made possible the fulfilment of the everlasting covenants with Abraham and David. As David wrote: *'Although my house is not so with God, Yet He has made with me an everlasting covenant, ordered in all things and secure. For this is all my salvation and all my desire; will He not make it increase?'* (2 Sam. 23:5)

God's covenant with David resonates strongly in this letter. We recall the promise to David that:

- God and David would share the paternity of Jesus

- that Jesus would be the builder of God's house

- that God would establish his throne and kingdom for ever

- that God would never take His mercy away from him.

The entire plan of salvation depended on the blood of Jesus and his resurrection by his Father.

May God make you complete

'May God… make you complete in every good work to do His will, working in you what is well pleasing in His sight, through Jesus Christ, to whom be glory forever and ever. Amen' (Heb. 13:21) Again, we have an example of Paul's prayers for his brothers and sisters, asking that God will work in them. We have looked at this topic under chapter 4. The Greek translated 'complete' (perfect in the A.V.) conveys the idea of repairing what is defective and of restoration. It reiterates the marvellous truth that our Father is doing everything possible to make His children fit for eternal companionship with His son. Our part is to place all our trust in Him and receive His works of repair gratefully.

A closing appeal

The letter is brought to a close with an appeal in this sublime final blessing: 'And I appeal to you, brethren, bear with the word of exhortation, for I have written to you in few words.' (Heb. 13:22) To put it in modern parlance: 'I do ask you, brothers, to take these words of advice kindly ; that is why I have written to you so briefly.' The content of the letter is so profound that it could have been a much longer letter. It was not necessary, however, because the Hebrews were so well versed in the Old Testament Scriptures. Hence, Paul could use spiritual shorthand, quoting from one Biblical source after another in order to prove the argument.

His appeal continues: *'Know that our brother Timothy has been set free, with whom I shall see you if he comes shortly. Greet all those who rule over you, and all the saints. Those from Italy greet you. Grace be with you all. Amen.'* (Heb. 13:23–25) It is evident that Paul knew many brothers and sisters in Rome; his letter to them mentions many of them in his greetings. Most were Gentiles, but some are referred to as fellow Jews. His reference to those of Italy greeting the Hebrews could suggest that Paul was staying with brothers and sisters outside Rome, perhaps those at Puteoli. On the other hand, it could refer to many from outside Rome who had visited him in his own hired house where he lived in chains under the palace guard.

He was hoping that now Timothy was free, presumably from prison, he would join Paul and they would travel together to Jerusalem. There they would meet the faithful elders. His hope would be that his letter would have re-established harmony in the ecclesia. However, we suggested above that this was not to be. His work was now finished and he would rest from his intense labours and sufferings for the Lord Jesus. Writing to Timothy he said: *'... the time of my departure is at hand. I have fought the good fight, I have finished the race, I have kept the faith. Finally, there is laid up for me the crown of righteousness, which the Lord, the righteous Judge, will give to me on that Day, and not to me only but also to all who have loved His appearing.'* (2 Tim. 4:6-8)

OTHER BOOKS AVAILABLE FROM DCP

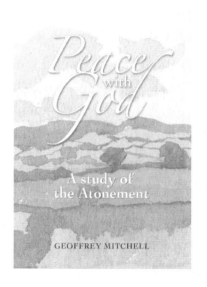

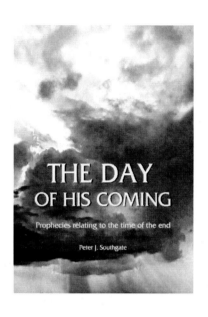

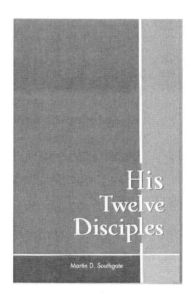

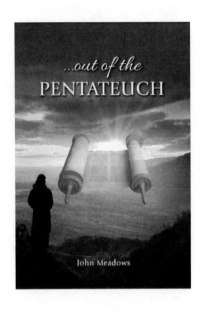

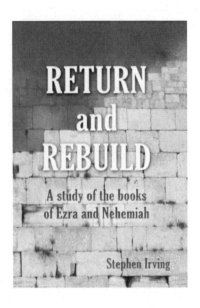

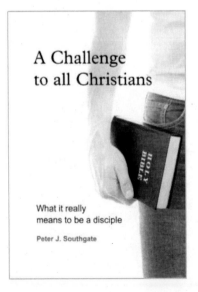